Sharing The Secret

Khalid Sohail

Jamie Lochlan

2021

Copyright

Published in 2021 by Green Zone Publishing
A division of Dr. Sohail MPC Inc.
213 Byron St. South
Whitby, Ontario Canada L1N 4P7
T. 905-666-7253   F. 905-666-4397
E-mail: welcome@drsohail.com
Website: www.drsohail.com

Sharing The Secret
Khalid Sohail, 1952 –
Jamie Lochlan, 1967 -

   1.   Psychotherapy   2. Sexual Abuse

ISBN: 978-1-927874-47-9

| Cover Design | Shahid Shafiq |
| Textual Design | Marcelina Naini |

"Dedicated to all those women and men who are silently suffering and reluctant to get professional help"

Table of Contents

INTRODUCTION

Letters Of Inspiration
By: Dr. Sohail

Dear Readers,

All around us, many girls and young women, as well as boys and young men are silently suffering because they were physically, emotionally and sexually abused as children, but they are reluctant to share their story and their secret as they are embarrassed. We still live with a taboo and stigma for people with emotional problems. Some survivors are experiencing symptoms of anxiety and depression, even suicidal ideas, because they have repressed their painful memories of past abuse.

Over the years I have met many therapists who are reluctant to work with patients with a history of sexual abuse.

I hope Jamie's story inspires young women and men to receive therapy and young therapists to help them, so that they can heal and grow, and lead a happy, healthy, and peaceful life that we call Green Zone Living.

Peacefully,

Dr. Sohail

Introduction

Sharing The Secret
By: Jamie Lochlan

It all started with a secret. One that never should have been kept. One I know couldn't escape …

I avoided the kind eyes of the man sitting in front of me. We had been sitting across from each other once a week for more years than I could count. Dr. Sohail had worked hard over the years to gain my trust; he had succeeded. But today I couldn't look into his kind eyes. I didn't want him to see my shame or the pain in them. I shifted nervously in my chair. My eyes burned. We were trying to figure out why I found it so difficult to make friends and why it was even harder for me to keep them. The more I thought about it; the clearer the answer became. It all went back to the secret. The one I hid from everyone in my day to day life. The one I wished I could hide from myself. The secret taught me two life lessons: 1. Trust no one and 2. I don't matter.

Both have kept me isolated and lonely. I'm not a recluse though. I have a family; a husband, children, mother, and in-laws. And even though I'm often surrounded by them, the secret and its lessons keep me very much alone. Through these letters between Dr. Sohail and myself, we will explore my relationships, my past and the secret together.

Sincerely,

Jamie

Letter 1 — Missing Pieces

Dear Dr. Sohail,

It's three in the morning and I've been struggling for the past four hours. I want to curl up in a ball and cry. I want to be held. I want to talk. But I'm alone. The only other person in the house is my husband but I can't talk to him, not about this. The door on that conversation closed decades ago. He would just tell me to leave it in the past and move on. But my past and present collide tonight, leaving me reeling with confusion and pain. I want to hurt myself to stop the pain, but I want to heal more. The band-aid that has held me together for the past twenty years is falling off.

The newest memory was triggered by a body memory. It's foggy but it's the missing piece of a previous memory. I'm about fifteen or sixteen, standing in my parents' kitchen. I'm panicky, wanting to escape. I'm not alone. He is there threatening me. But I'm not a little kid anymore. I can protect myself. I let him know that. He shoves me to the floor and pins me down. I'm on my back. He finally lets me get up. I don't know what he did. My memory is blank. He sneers at me and lets me know that he can get to me any time he wants. I'll never be safe. He leaves and I grab a steak knife from the drawer and hold it to my wrist. I want to die.

I've always wondered what happened to make me hold a blade to my wrist. Was it just the threat of him being able to hurt me any time he wanted or was it something more? It must have been bad. And why did my mind only let me retrieve part of the memory? Why won't it let me remember what he did?

Tonight I got the missing piece of the memory. It's foggy but I can see what happened. It's playing in my mind like an old projector film. After he pinned me down, he flipped me over onto my stomach, yanked my jeans down and raped me anally. When he climbed off me, I tugged my jeans back up and sat on the floor, crying. Then he tells me that he can get to me any time. He sneers at me and leaves. I jump up and grab a steak knife out of the drawer. I slid down and sit on the floor with my back against the cupboard. I'm crying and holding the knife to my wrist. I want to die. I don't want him to hurt me again.

I thought the worst of the abuse stopped when I was about ten, but I was wrong. My mind is reeling.

It's now the following day. My head still feels foggy. I flip between feeling numb and feeling hurt. The emotional pain is so deep that it cuts me to my core. I'm struggling to make it through the day.

A week later, the fog has finally lifted. But the pain is still there. My mind refuses to think about the new memory or the information it provided. But I have to think about it and talk about it in order to heal. How do I get through this, Dr. Sohail?

Sincerely,

Jamie

Letter 2 — Trust

Dear Jamie

I feel honoured that your trust in our therapeutic relationship has grown to the level that you are able to write your first letter and share your secret with me.

I am well aware that it was not easy for you to trust a therapist, especially a male therapist, with such intimate details of your life because as a child you had trusted the man that betrayed your trust. It took us a long time to build a trusting relationship.

Over the years I offered you Supportive Therapy. I listened to your ongoing family challenges and social struggles, and offered you reassurance so that you could cope with your day to day life.

Over the years I noticed a pattern in your lifestyle. I noticed that it was difficult for you to initiate and then maintain close relationships.

Now that both your children have become teenagers and are getting ready to leave the nest, I wanted you to create a circle of friends that I call "Family of the Heart".

I also realized that you were ready to graduate from Supportive Therapy to Dynamic Therapy. That is why I suggested that we review your present and past relationships so that you can uncover your unconscious patterns and become aware of your conscious difficulties in creating close connections with people.

Dear Jamie,

I am not surprised that you had a new memory about your past abuse. That means you have become a deep sea diver in your unconscious mind to bring back a memory that had been buried there for a long time. I know such memories are painful, but they are also liberating. They are like labour pains that help you deliver your new self, your healthy self and your enlightened self. You are ready now to create a peaceful lifestyle and healthy relationships.

I am also aware that you are not comfortable sharing your painful memories with your friends and relatives, but fortunately you trust me enough to share them with me.

I want to reassure you that I am here to help you and support you to heal and recover and grow to your fullest potential. I have been telling you that you are a wonderful writer and you can write your story in such a way that it can inspire many people, especially women who have suffered because of physical, emotional and sexual abuse. You are now ready to write the next chapter of your life in the form of letters. Therapy can be seen as rewriting your life story as an adult, in which you are the hero and not the victim. Can you share with me what were the circumstances when you had to see a psychiatrist for the first time in your life and what was the outcome of that meeting?

Peacefully,

Dr. Sohail

Letter 3 — The Journey Begins

Dear Dr. Sohail,

I am glad you are willing to take this journey with me. I know it's not going to be an easy, but with your help and support I can do it. We can explore my relationships and the secret that still influences my daily life.

I was just twenty years old when I decided to seek professional help for the first time. At the time I was doing my Masters degree in journalism and struggling with living away from my family for the first time. I missed my mom terribly since we are very close. I was in a very demanding course and under a lot of pressure to pass. I was under academic probation for the first three months of the course because my American undergrad degree was deemed insufficient by the Canadian University. I had a lot to prove. As the stress of living on my own and pressure to succeed grew, so did my depression. I was becoming suicidal. Adding to my depression was my overwhelming need to check the door locks, stove dials, taps and electrical appliances to ensure that they were either locked or off so that I was safe. It got so bad that I would not leave my bachelor apartment unless I had class. Sometimes when the checking behaviour was too much, I would skip class and call in sick. I rejected any invitations to hangout or party with my classmates.

One day I was walking across the university grounds and I was feeling more depressed and desperate than usual. I started thinking of ways to hurt myself when I got back to my apartment. Lately, I couldn't walk past the cutlery drawer without pausing and resisting the urge to grab a sharp knife to hurt myself with. I couldn't stand the checking behaviours any longer and the pressure of school. Why was my mind so messed up? Why couldn't I stop checking? It was stupid. Normal people didn't check those things, not to the same extent that I did. I suddenly realized that I needed help or I would probably end up hurting myself. I turned around and started walking toward the counselling center. It took every ounce of strength I had to walk up to the desk and request to see a counsellor. The middle aged lady behind the counter explained that Dr. C was a psychiatrist and she could see me next week. I took the appointment, but for the next few days, I considered cancelling. Was I really that sick that I needed to see a shrink? Sure I was going through a rough time, but I could handle it, right? I also worried that the shrink would think that I was crazy and commit me to a hospital. Then bye-bye school and I would disappoint my parents and the former university professor who had helped me get into the Masters program. I was also scared about how my boyfriend of five years would feel about me getting hospitalized. That was way more than he signed on for.

The week passed very slowly. Somehow I found the courage to keep the appointment. Dr. C was an older woman, maybe late fifties or early sixties. She was nice and tried to make me feel comfortable. I naively wondered why she didn't wear a white doctor's coat. She was a doctor after all. Dr. C tried to get me to open up but I remained guarded. I told her about missing my mom and family, that I found school very stressful and that I was having trouble sleeping at night. But the whole time I talked with her, I was very careful and reminded myself that anything I said could give her reason to have me committed to a mental hospital. She had that power. I was scared that she was analyzing every word I said, looking for the crack in my armour and looking for symptoms of mental illness. It took a few months before I trusted her enough to tell her that I was depressed. I didn't admit to feeling suicidal, but I think she suspected that and encouraged me to book extra appointments or call the helpline if I needed to. I never told her about my checking behaviours. I thought if I described the overwhelming need to check and the horrible anxiety that I felt if I didn't do it, that she would perceive me as crazy. I thought I was crazy so why wouldn't she. I wanted to tell her about it. I wanted to tell her how bad it made me feel about myself and that I hated myself for checking. There were days I wanted to die just so I didn't have to check another damn door lock. I wanted to tell her about the deep emotional pain that I felt every day. But we barely scratched the surface of the emotional hell that I was in. With Dr. C's support I finished my program and got my degree. I was now ready to start the next phase of my life-getting married and starting a life with my soon-to-be husband. But the pain refused to go away...

That's my first experience of seeing a psychiatrist. But it wasn't my last. My experience with Dr. C taught me that psychiatrists weren't as scary as I thought. She was nice, kind and compassionate. I regret not opening up to her. Maybe she could have helped me if I had only given her a chance. Maybe all of the pain that followed could have been prevented if I had opened up. But I wasn't ready. It took a long time ...

Sincerely,

Jamie

Letter 4 — Leaving Home

Dear Jamie,

I would like to thank you for having such confidence in our therapeutic relationship. You know very well that I genuinely care for your health and happiness. I always believed that human beings grow in the womb of caring relationships whether personal, family or professional.

Leaving home for the first time can be a challenging experience. Many experience separation anxiety and if there is an extra pressure of the studies at the university and fitting in with the crowd, it can cause an emotional crisis. There are so many students who experience their first nervous breakdown when they leave home and enter university. Your two emotional conditions, your Depression and your Obsessive Compulsive Disorder made each other worse. You were wise enough to get psychiatric care and you were lucky to have an older motherly or grandmotherly psychiatrist who was kind, caring and considerate. Don't be hard on yourself as it is never easy to bare one's soul in front of a stranger because it can be very embarrassing.

You are well aware that we live in a culture where mental illness is a stigma. Psychiatrists are called *shrinks* and patients are called *lunatics*. It is understandable that you were nervous about sharing your personal and intimate details to a stranger. I am glad Dr. C helped you complete your studies and get ready to be married.

Dear Jamie,

You have shared with me in the past that you were admitted to Whitby Psychiatric Hospital. After seeing Dr. C, did you have to see other psychiatrists or therapists before you were admitted to the hospital?

For the readers of these letters can you share how you spend your week these days and what have been your passions? That will help them connect the dots of your past, present and future. Do you have plans for the future and how do you relate to your family?

I am looking forward to your next letter.

Peacefully,

Dr. Sohail

Letter 5 — A Desperate Cry For Help

Dear Dr. Sohail,

This week I feel like I've been drowning in memories as I go through all my old notes, papers and books to determine which to pack or discard. My husband and I bought a new house and it is a very daunting task to pack up twenty years of stuff that we accumulated in our current house. Fortunately, the deadline is several months away. During my purging of the clutter, I found old diaries and notes from what feels like a previous life.

I remember telling you about my admission to Whitby Psychiatric Hospital that happened when I was twenty six years old. I did have to seek help prior to my admission there.

After I graduated and got married, my husband D and I moved to Toronto where he got a job. We found a really nice basement apartment and began our life together. I applied for jobs, wrote my first novel and took care of our little kitten Casey that we adopted. Life would have been great had it not been for the uncontrollable checking behaviours and my growing depression. Unable to find a job in my field of journalism, I took a part-time job in a pet store to occupy my time and continued writing my Young Adults' novel. We adopted a second cat named Troubles to keep our cat Casey company. My depression grew as my search for a job in my field became more difficult. The checking behaviours got worse too. I had trouble checking the stove and locking the apartment to go to work and trouble locking up the store after work.

Everything came to a head one evening. My husband and I rushed through dinner, threw the dishes in the sink and hurried out the door to drive to our friend's house. As we drove along, I asked my husband if the stove was off to which he replied, "Fry cats ... I mean bye cats." I lost it. "Go back", I yelled, but D refused. Filled with panic and fear for my cats, I tried opening the door of the moving car to jump out and run back to the apartment. After that we both knew that I needed serious help. D got me connected with a psychologist from his Employers Assistance Program. The psychologist asked me a lot of questions and after a few sessions he referred me to a psychiatrist at the nearest hospital.

Going to the hospital for therapy was pretty frightening. After exiting the elevator door, the locked inpatient ward was on one side and the other side was the outpatient unit, including the day treatment program. I sat in the waiting area for my name to be called. It took all of my strength to not run back into the elevator and leave. A petite lady wearing a nice blouse and leather mini skirt walked into the waiting area. She called my name. I followed her down the hall into her office. She introduced herself. Dr. M asked me questions about my depression, the checking behaviors, how I was sleeping, etc. I left with a prescription, the first of many and a weekly appointment. Those early sessions are a blur, probably from all the medication I was taking. I was first put on Anafranil for depression and Obsessive Compulsive

Disorder (O.C.D.) and Xanax for anxiety. When I was twenty four, I was hospitalized for depression and suicidal ideation. Then my medications were changed to Prozac for depression, Lithium for mood swings, and Desipramine for depression. I was put into a day treatment program. I became friends with one of the patients. We used to joke that it was "better to be in red than dead," referring to the red hospital gowns worn by the inpatients. I ended up being hospitalized again for a second time.

This hospitalization was very different from the first. The urge to hurt myself was very strong one night and the nurses refused to talk to me. The nurse assigned to me told me to go back to my room and wait for my session in the morning. I broke a plastic cassette box and used the sharp side to cut my wrist. It didn't do much but made an angry look red welt on my wrist. I think it was the next day when the ward psychiatrist told me he was discharging me. I protested that I wasn't ready to leave the hospital and that I still felt very suicidal. He told me that I "just need to grow up." D took me home and stayed home from work for the rest of the week so he could protect me from myself. I finished my stint in day treatment and returned to my weekly session with Dr. M.

The weekly sessions were nothing more than me telling her how much I wanted to die followed by her increasing my medication or adding new ones. She put me on Anafranil for depression, Prozac for depression, Lithium for mood swings, Xanax for anxiety, and Clonazepam for sleeping. I was prescribed all of these pills for daily use. I was in such a drugged state that it was surprising that I could find my way home. She didn't seem interested in actually helping me. She blamed my parents for my depression. I knew that my childhood was not rosy, but my parents loved me and did the best they could. They weren't responsible for the horrible pain that I felt deep within my soul. I felt on almost a cellular level that something was horribly wrong, but I didn't know what it was. It went beyond the difficult childhood and the OCD.

At age twenty six, I saw Dr. M for the last time. During our session, I told her that I would not be returning for our session next week, that I had had enough of the pain. I knew that she could call in the orderlies to escort me to the locked ward. I had seen this happen before and I knew that it was within her power. The week before I had brought in a pocket knife, that I had bought and told her that I planned to use it on my wrists. She asked me to hand her the knife and she put it in her desk drawer. I didn't need the pocket knife this time because I had another plan. She wasn't interested in hearing my cries for help. She just kept insisting that I return next week and brings D with me. She increased my medication. I told her that she would never see me again. I walked to the office door, opened it and left. She did not try to stop me.

I took the GO train home, jumped in my car and drove down to the lake. I had hidden a exacto knife blades in the back of the car. When I got to the lake, I took a blade and walked down the embankment to the waters' edge. I sat there for the longest time thinking about my husband and my parents and in-laws, and my two cats. I thought they would be better off without me. I didn't matter to my own psychiatrist who could not be bothered to stop me from leaving her office while I threatened suicide. As I held the blade to my wrist, a man stood on the embankment and yelled down to me, "Do you know what time it is?" I froze and yelled back, "No." He thanked me and left. He could not even take the time to see that another human being was trying to end her life. More proof that I didn't matter. I made the cut lengthwise down my forearm, not across like in the movies. Lengthwise is harder to stitch up and more effective. But the blade was dull and it wouldn't cut deep enough. I had two choices: go home and get another blade or go for help. One single thought crossed my mind, "what if things could get better?" I decided to go for help.

I drove to my doctors' office. When I got to the reception desk, the receptionist asked me what I needed to see the doctor about. I removed the jacket that I had wrapped around my bloody wrist and showed her. She quickly escorted me into a room and ran to get my doctor. After the doctor examined and cleaned my cut wrist. She matter-of-factly said, "I can't let you go after what you've just done. I can give you two choices; go back to the general hospital where your psychiatrist works or I can send you to the local Psychiatric Hospital?" I told her that I never wanted to go back to that hospital and would prefer the psychiatric hospital so that's how I ended up there.

And that's where the story really gets interesting …

Sincerely,

Jamie

Letter 6 — Psychotherapy And Medication: Their Roles

Dear Jamie,

I am so glad you are able to continue this written dialogue. I am hopeful that it will not only help you heal and help you develop some insights in your past, but also inspire you to make wise choices in the future. People say one cannot change one's past, but in therapy when we review the past we change it by giving it a new meaning. In therapy, we rewrite the past as a healthy and strong adult rather than as a weak and vulnerable victim.

By reading your letter I realized how seriously your Obsessive Compulsive Disorder (O.C.D) has affected your life in the past.

Dear Jamie,

Some traditional doctors and psychiatrists only use medications to help their psychiatric patients. For me medications have been the last, not the first line of treatment. I try to help my patients with psychotherapy so that they develop a better understanding of their unconscious, self-destructive patterns and be able to learn healthy coping mechanisms of life. In my opinion, medications can help patients control their symptoms of anxiety, depression and insomnia, but they do not help them deal with underlying feelings of loneliness or a sense of failure in their personal, social and professional relationships.

In our clinic we use combination therapy: a combination of individual, marital, family and group therapy. I do prescribe medications when needed, but most of my patients are not on any medications and many cut them down after they started therapy with me.

I felt sad reading that your psychiatrist did not pick on your serious intent to hurt yourself and felt glad to read that at the final moment of decision, you chose life over death and chose to get professional help to not only live but also improve your quality of life and love.

Now I am curious to know who introduced you to the Psychotherapy Unit and what were your experiences with your therapists?

I am looking forward to this letter exchange.

Peacefully,

Dr. Sohail

Letter 7 — Choices

Dear Dr. Sohail,

The Obsessive Compulsive Disorder really affected my life in the past. It was crippling at times. Even today it still affects me, but not to the same extent. I can go out without being paralyzed by the checking behaviours. It just takes me a lot longer than anyone else to lock the door. My nightly ritual of checking the stove, door locks, and windows takes way more time than I want to admit, but I eventually get it done and go to bed. It is something I've learned to live with and not beat myself up over. A therapist once told me a long time ago that OCD can be a symptom of childhood sexual abuse. I didn't want to believe her then because I had no memories of the abuse. But I believe her now. My memories didn't start to surface until I was about twenty seven years old and was being treated in the Psychotherapy Program at the Psychiatric Hospital.

Prior to my admission to the Psychotherapy Program, I was admitted to the Admissions ward for diagnosis. When I got there, I was greeted by a tough, no-nonsense nurse named Sandy who searched me and informed me that she would officially put me on a non-voluntary hold if I tried to leave, it was my choice. Sandy wasn't fooling around. I thought to myself, "finally someone who cared enough to protect me from myself. Maybe I could finally get the help I needed." I agreed to stay. While on the admission ward, the same nurse challenged me on a regular basis. One day she asked me, "How much longer do you think it will be before your husband and family have to walk away because they can't bear to see you hurt yourself any more?" I thought about what life without my husband and family would look like, and I didn't like it; it scared me. I still felt suicidal, but instead of hurting myself I would talk to my nurse. Sandy was still tough on me, but I felt that she genuinely cared about me too.

One night the reality of being on a locked psychiatric ward hit me hard. A female patient a few years younger than me told me to avoid the bathroom around three in the morning. Not wanting to get caught up in any trouble, I stayed away from her and the bathroom. When I could not wait any longer, I walked down the hall to the bathroom around four in the morning. I went in and there was dried blood on the floor. As I exited the bathroom, I saw the girl in the hall, holding a compress to her forearm. She smiled at me and pulled the compress away to reveal a long jagged cut down the inside of her forearm. I hurried back to my room. The next morning when I saw her I asked her why she hurt herself. I was expecting her to say that she did it because she couldn't stand the pain anymore. The answer I got shook me to my core. She did it to give her nurse a hard time because he had taken away her ground privileges. To her it was just a game. A very sad and twisted game. I felt sorry for her nurse who seemed to genuinely want to help her. I asked her where she got the blade since every patient entering the unit is searched for such items. She smiled and told me to follow her into the washroom. She entered a stall, reached above the window frame and grabbed a rusty razor blade. "But how did you get it in here without the nurses finding it?" I asked. She replied that she had hid it in her vagina and then said that I could use it any time. I was repulsed and stunned. I rushed out of the washroom and avoided her after that. That was a whole new level of sickness that I vowed to never attain.

Later when the unit psychiatrist asked me if I wanted a "Band-Aid or a solution" to my problems, I eagerly replied, "Solution. I already tried Band-Aids and they don't work. I need a solution because otherwise I'll keep doing this until I get it right and die." The solution he offered me was a nine months stay in the hospitals Psychotherapy Program. He said he had seen the staff there do incredible work in helping patients turn their lives around. Patients on that unit had to be off all medication and not use alcohol or drugs. They lived on the unit during the week and were able to go home on weekends. To get accepted into the program, I had to go off all my meds and not hurt myself. I also had to stay on the admissions ward if I wanted to get into the Program faster. The Unit Psychiatrist joked that "we have to get you out of here soon because if you are not crazy coming in, you will be if you stay too long."

It was a very long three weeks until I got transferred to the Psychotherapy Program. Sandy remained tough on me. She kept reminding me that any self-harm attempt would cancel my application to the Psychotherapy Unit. She encouraged me to reach out when I felt suicidal. She kept telling me that "you are young and smart. This doesn't have to be your life." On nights when the urge to hurt myself was overwhelming, this incredible woman would talk me down and remind me that with help from the Psychotherapy Program, I could have a real life. I didn't give up and neither did she.

I didn't make it easy for Sandy though. When I asked her why she didn't just let me "off myself," her words somehow cut through my pain. "I can't stop you if you really want to kill yourself because you will end up doing it anyway once you are out of here. I can only help you if you want my help. I know you're really hurting and you want the pain to stop. If you let us, we can help you, but we cannot help you if you are dead." On another night when the urge to hurt myself was overwhelming and I was pacing in my room, I thought about smashing the window to get a piece of glass but didn't know if I could get a piece through the wire mesh covering the glass. Sandy walked in and saw me. I told her that I was planning to smash the glass and use it to hurt myself. Her reply caught me off guard. "Fine, but the hospital will have to bill you for the cost of replacing it," she said. Consequences were a foreign concept. Most psych patients get a pass on their behaviour because they are psych patients. The thought of being held responsible for my actions was startling at best. This was a first, but the concept of consequences would come up frequently later on. Now that she had my attention, she got me to open up about why I was so upset. Last night I was very suicidal and had tried to talk to another nurse but he told me to wait until morning to talk with my nurse. He didn't want to hear anything I had to say and didn't care that I was feeling suicidal. He threatened to lock me up in the isolation room if I did not go back to my room. I learned that I had to seek out people like Sandy who wanted to help me and to avoid people like this jerk.

Dr. Sohail, looking back, I realize now that there were defining moments in my life where I had to choose. By the water with the razor blade in my hand, I chose to get help rather than continue. In the admissions ward, I chose to trust my nurse and open up to her and let her help me. I clearly saw the revolving door of hospitalizations and medications that I was falling into until I either got the help I needed or succeeded in suicide. There were days when I wanted to die, but I realize now that I just wanted to be free of the pain. I wanted someone to help me and to care about me. I wanted to matter. The admission ward nurse and the psychiatrist cared enough to offer real help and real caring. They made a difference and got me on the right track. That track was the Psychotherapy Program.

I wrote *"SHORE OF NOWHERE"* about my suicide attempt and how I felt at that time. It was the first in a long line of poems.

SHORE OF NOWHERE

A freezing rain

Revives me

For a time

As I stand

On the shore

Of nowhere

Thinking

Of the line

Between

Life and death.

Singing along

With the song

In my mind

I embrace its

Rhythm and rhyme

That ease the pain

But only

For a time.

Pushing the song

From my mind

I go back

To the line.

As waves break

Upon the shore

I yell

"No more"

To an uncaring sky

That watches while

The rest of me

Dr. K Sohail and Jamie Lochlan

Dies

As I lie

On the shore

Of nowhere.

Sincerely,

Jamie

Letter 8 — Time for Medication

Dear Dr. Sohail,

I'm so glad you only prescribe medication to help with therapy and not in place of it, like so many other psychiatrists. The doctor that I saw before being admitted to the Psychiatric hospital used it as the primary means of therapy; talk therapy was minimal. The day treatment psychiatrist was a very nice man, but his main focus was drug-based treatment too. You are the first psychiatrist that I've met whose majority of patients are not on meds and who focuses more on talk therapy than medication.

When we first met all those years ago, I was very much against psychotropic medication. I had been discharged a few years earlier from the Psychotherapy Unit which forbade the use of meds. As a result, my opinion on using psychotropic medication was that I didn't need it nor want it. My experience with the first psychiatrist who had me taking numerous meds which left me in a constant fog reinforced my determination to never take that type of medication again.

We worked together for several years before you brought up the topic of medication. I was very opposed to it. I felt that antidepressants made me lose control and act on suicidal feelings. Being a mother with two young children, I could not afford to lose control and act on those feelings. I owed it to my children to be there for them. Unfortunately, my depression was getting worse as was my temper. I was quick to anger which scared me and was not normally part of my nature. I was also having self-harm thoughts which scared me even more. I was taught at the Psychotherapy Unit that it's okay to have those feelings, just not okay to act on them. I told you that I was afraid that my depression would get out of control and I could act on those feelings. You brought up the topic of medication and this time I listened.

You told me that you thought I was Cyclothymic, which is the mildest form of Bipolar Disorder and explained that my mood swings would benefit from a mood stabilizer and not an antidepressant. An antidepressant would actually make things worse for me which it had in the past. While on Prozac and other antidepressants, I was not able to stop myself from acting on self-harm thoughts and ended up hospitalized three times. I researched Cyclothymia and its symptoms struck a chord. Maybe I was Cyclothymic. I was feeling desperate and afraid again. Even though I was against medication, I trusted you to help me. I agreed to try a mood stabilizer, Carbamazepine. It gradually levelled me out. I didn't feel out of control like I had with antidepressants. It made the crushing lows, not as low. I never really felt that manic high, just felt up and happy, and never out of control. The medication helped me maintain a balance and kept my temper even.

To this day, I still take Carbamazepine and it still helps. I don't feel out of control, and even when I get depressed, it doesn't last as long or hit as hard. I can lead a normal life. My husband and I raised two incredible, intelligent, caring, responsible children who are now young adults pursuing their own lives and loves. I haven't been hospitalized for depression in over twenty five years.

But being able to lead a normal life isn't just about getting the medication right, there is so much more that happened …

Sincerely,

Jamie

Letter 9 — Defence And Coping Mechanisms

Dear Jamie,

I am so glad you are continuing to share different chapters of your story in the form of letters highlighting your struggles and successes, dilemmas and dreams.

In your letter you shared the painful story of a female patient who slashed her arm to get back at her therapist. In psychiatric terms we call it acting out. Rather than going back to her nurse and sharing her disappointment and acting inside the relationship, she acted outside the relationship. For mental health professionals, acting out is an immature defence mechanism to cope with emotional conflicts.

Dear Jamie,

Since we are considering publishing these letters one day to educate the public about mental health and psychotherapy, let me share the concept of defence and coping mechanisms that we learnt from Sigmund Freud.

Freud believed in a hierarchy of defence and coping mechanisms. Children use different mechanisms to cope with anxiety than teenagers and adults. As human beings mature their coping mechanisms also mature. When an adult uses the defence mechanisms of a child or a teenager, we consider that immature. We also see different defence mechanisms in action in different clinical conditions. Let me share a few examples to elaborate my point.

People suffering from schizophrenia use projection and suffer from delusions. Rather than saying ...I hate him....a woman might project on her husband and say...he hates me.

People suffering from Bipolar Disorder use denial. Patient's mother dies and he laughs as he is not willing to accept the pain of separation and death. Rather than feeling sad he feels euphoric which is like reaction formation.

People with personality problems use acting out like the female patient you mentioned.

Alongside immature and unhealthy defence mechanisms, there are also healthy and mature coping mechanisms.

Freud considered humour and sublimation as mature coping mechanisms. In humour a person shares his painful feelings without offending the other person. In sublimation a person finds a socially accepting method for his or her socially unacceptable need or desire. For example someone who wants to drive fast becomes an ambulance driver or a man who has too much aggression becomes a boxer or a woman who wants to expose herself becomes a dancer or an actress. These are different examples of sublimation.

Dear Jamie,

I am so glad that in difficult times you made wise choices. You opted for long term therapy over band-aid solutions and chose life over death. I am so happy that you are alive to share your story and inspire others through your writings to make wise, healthy and mature choices in life.

I am looking forward to your professional experiences and existential encounters in the psychotherapy unit.

Peacefully,

Dr. Sohail

Letter 10 — Struggle For Tomorrow

Dear Dr. Sohail

I saw a lot of acting out through the years; patients who didn't know how or didn't want to change their lives for the better. They held onto the behaviours that they knew would get them attention, not necessarily true help. To get real help, they had to want to work on their issues and their behaviour. I learned this while in the Psychotherapy Program. I witnessed patients who said they wanted to get better, but they would violate one of the rules like no alcohol or drug use, no self-harm and end up being removed from the program. I've worked hard on my issues and truly wanted to get better. But there are times when past feelings and present feelings collide.

Lately, I've been struggling a lot. And those acting out behaviours that you mention ... Well, I have to keep reminding myself why they are not okay and to find healthy ways of coping with my depression and frustration.

Dr. K Sohail and Jamie Lochlan

When I left the Psychotherapy program, I thought the attraction to self-harm would diminish and eventually go away. But it drops in like an old friend and taunts me from time to time. These past few weeks have been very difficult. Most days when I should be packing and decluttering the house to prepare for moving in the spring, I end up sitting at the kitchen table for hours, playing on my phone and losing time until my back gets sore from sitting too long and brings me back to the present. At night I lose myself in depression and feel so down that I want to cry. It brings me back to how I felt twenty five years ago, while at the Psychotherapy program. I felt alone, hurting, depressed and frustrated. Although the feelings are not as strong; they are not mild either. Depression has a good hold on me. It's like a thick, dark, heavy blanket that wraps itself around me, so I can't breathe, can't see and can't move. I'm at its mercy. There is no sunlight; no hope. That's how I've been feeling. I just wrote *"STRUGGLE FOR TOMORROW"*

Struggle For Tomorrow

Will a broken mind

Ever mend.

Will a shattered soul

Breathe again.

Standing on the end

Of a past that won't let me live.

Suspended between now and then

I struggle for tomorrow.

And old friend

You've heard my sorrow.

Right on cue

You tell me to

Pick up the blade

And end tomorrow.

I should push you away

But you'd only return

Another day

To call me home.

Dr. K Sohail and Jamie Lochlan

When I decided to get pregnant twenty three years ago and have my first child, I made the conscious decision that, from that moment on, suicide would no longer be an option. I have not made a suicide attempt since my last hospitalization twenty five years ago. But to be honest, it does cross my mind when I'm overwhelmed by depression or OCD or memories of the abuse. I can't help it. When I'm feeling really bad, sometimes it's the only thing that comforts me, knowing that I could opt out. It would be my choice, but I fight the pull to commit suicide, and instead accept the lesser version; self-harm as a consideration. That pull can be very strong too. But I fight it too. I hear my therapist, Kathy, from the Psychotherapy program's voice in my head. She told me that there could be times in my life when I feel suicidal or feel like hurting myself, and "It's okay to have those feelings, it's just not okay to act on them." *

The depression is so bad that I've considered not taking my carbamazepine. I know that if I miss a few doses, I will feel a little euphoric and a little manic. Maybe this will pull me out of my depression.

My mood today was a little better and I was actually able to function today. I hope it lasts. But my mind still feels muddled, like it's swimming through sludge. I just want to sleep. Feeling very tired tonight. And I feel sad because both of my young adult children want to move out as soon as possible because they don't like living at home. I feel like I've failed them. The happy home that I tried so hard to build has crumbled like a house of cards. I'll try to write more tomorrow. Dr. Sohail. I can't write anymore tonight.

Sincerely,

Jamie

Letter 11 — Progress Is Not Linear

Dear Jamie,

I remember the times when patients were discharged from the Psychotherapy Unit because they had broken some rules and were sent to me for follow-up in the Outpatient Department. Psychotherapy Unit staff knew that I liked offering psychotherapy to people struggling with personality problems.

Dear Jamie,

I realize that you are going through a rough time, a difficult phase in your life. I think you are temporarily regressing because

...your children are planning to leave home

...you are planning to sell your house and buy a new one

and

...you are engaging in dynamic therapy which is stirring up old and painful memories.

Let me reassure you at this stage. Your regression is temporary. Over the years you have matured and learned many coping mechanisms to control your self-destructive thoughts and not act on them. With dynamic therapy the more you deal with your unresolved issues successfully, the more you will feel stronger. Have you not heard what does not kill you makes you stronger.

Over the years and decades as a practicing psychotherapist I have learnt that progress does not take place in a straight line. Three steps forward, one step back. But even when you are taking one step back you are still far ahead than where you started. Over the years I have seen you grow as a loving mother and a creative writer. You have become a stronger human being and now you can deal with your day to day life and with any family crisis gracefully and respectfully and peacefully.

In the last few years I have seen you invest a lot of time, money and energy in your son's creativity and music. Now I would like you to invest in your own creative writing so that when he flies from the nest, you will have your own creative projects to pursue. Otherwise, you will go through separation anxiety and depression. I would like to help you prepare for your grown up children leaving the nest. The idea of letter exchange is one step in that direction.

I am curious about your stay in the Psychotherapy Unit. How long did you stay and what did you learn?

I am thoroughly enjoying this letter exchange and impressed how you are reflecting on your past and articulating your story, a story that will help and inspire many readers, especially young women.

Peacefully,

Dr. Sohail

Letter 12 — Mixed State

Dear Dr. Sohail,

This week has been up and down. My depression has been manageable. Through the years I've learned that I just need to hold on and let the depression run its course and I will eventually start to feel better. I didn't stop taking my mood stabilizer because I realized that although it might pull my mood up, the ensuing crash would not be worth it. I just held on, like I have so many times before.

I think I'm in a mixed state now because my mood swings from okay to being depressed. I received good news about my son's music career so things are looking up on that front. Hopefully it will lead to something bigger for him and he can advance his career. My in-laws also came for a visit and to help get the house ready to sell. We got a lot of painting and odd jobs done so that has lessened my stress a bit. My daughter is having trouble finding a full time job and her best friend ended their sixteen year friendship suddenly.

I'm worried about her and spend a lot of time talking and comforting her. I hope she knows that I'm always there for her; at least I try to be. I don't ever want her to feel that she is alone with her problems, like I felt at her age. I'm focussing on her and acting like I'm fine. Truth be told; I'm not fine. I hate being in a mixed state because my moods change so rapidly at times it's like being in a washing machine, jumping between soak and spin. It saps my energy. My mind feels sharp and foggy at the same time, kind of like a camera that keeps trying to focus. I feel overwhelmed at times.

Both my kids said their dad and I are the reason they want to move out. They hate living with us. I am devastated by this. I feel I failed them. I tried so hard to make our home a loving place for them to grow up and to feel safe in, but I failed miserably. I am crushed. If they had said that they want to move out to have their freedom, I could understand that. But they said it was because of my "idiosyncrasies" as they put it and because of their father and his behaviour. I gave my whole adult life to care for them and now I realize that they don't appreciate it or even acknowledge it. I wanted to give them everything, but it was never good enough. I was never good enough. That's how it feels. I've always felt that way.

When I walked through the doors of the Psychotherapy Program, I felt worthless, alone, depressed and desperate. I was just twenty six years old but I was already close to giving up on life. This was my last chance. When I met my prime therapist Kathy, I wasn't ready to trust anyone and open up to them. But she managed to put a small chink in my armor during our very first meeting. Kathy was professional and calm with a gentle voice and caring gleam in her eyes. When she told me, "We're here to help you, if you let us. I want to help you,"* I believed her. I needed and wanted her to care about me. I wanted her to help me. For the first time in my life, there was a glimmer of hope.

I didn't make it easy for Kathy or for my associate therapist Beth. There are lots to tell about my nine months in the Psychotherapy Program. I'll have to save it for my next letter.

Sincerely,

Jamie

Letter 13 — Resilience

Dear Jamie,

I am so glad you are feeling better. You are becoming resilient and learning to cope with your dark phases of life without losing hope and hurting yourself. You know now that...it will also pass.

I think you are hard on yourself as a mother. I have seen for years that you have been a kind and caring, nurturing and loving mother to them. Their father has been a bit strict though setting limits and they do not like that as teenagers. Many teenagers hate authority. Henry Miller, the famous and notorious novelist once said, "We hate our parents to liberate ourselves."

Your children are getting ready to leave the nest and they are finding excuses to leave home. Do not take it to heart. I am confident once they leave they will miss you and come back to tell you how much they love you. I am worried about you and trying to help you to learn to cope with an empty nest. I want you to have your own hobby and passion and a small circle of friends so that you can enjoy your life once your mothering role is over.

I am looking forward to reading your experiences in the Psychotherapy Unit and finding out how you transformed your breakdown into a breakthrough.

Peacefully,

Dr. Sohail

Letter 14 — Trust And Truth

Dear Dr. Sohail,

I didn't realize it at the time but being at the Psychotherapy Program was the start of a new chapter in my life; one that would put me on the path to healing from a childhood trauma that I didn't even know had happened.

The first step in dealing with that trauma was learning to trust and open up to my two therapists, Kathy and Beth. I had to take these initial risks before I could feel safe enough to remember the trauma itself.

I remember the first time I opened up to Kathy. Kathy had noticed at the start of our session that I was upset and said that I looked like I was about to cry. The tenderness in her voice and look of concern in her eyes touched me. And although my instincts were telling me not to trust anyone with my feelings, I decided to take a risk. I told her about how my previous psychiatrist let me walk out of her office and insisted that I would return, but I insisted that she would never see me again.

"She could have suggested hospitalization or even had me committed, but she didn't do anything.* She didn't give a damn about me," I told Kathy. "I just needed her to care enough to protect me from myself," I admitted to Kathy. "I don't matter," I cried. "I'm just worthless." Kathy looked into my eyes and in a gentle, caring voice told me something that she would repeat numerous times throughout my hospital stay. "You matter." And it took the full nine months of Kathy saying it, for it to sink and for me to start believing it.

The first time I opened up to Beth was not by choice. I had been struggling with a memory that I couldn't make sense out of. It was an image of hands moving toward my private area. The image kept playing in my mind. It could have been what I saw when the doctor set my broken leg in traction when I was nine. But for some reason, it felt more sinister than that. I felt that something was horribly wrong and could not escape that feeling. I was hiding in my bed, feeling young and scared. When I was late for my session with Beth, she came and got me from my bed. She told me to meet her in the meeting room. When I joined her in the meeting room, I quickly slid onto the couch and tightly hugged my stuffed rabbit. *Beth immediately realized that something was wrong and proceeded with caution. She gently asked me, "Who is your little friend?"

Pulling the stuffed animal closer, I stuttered, "Thumper."

"You're safe here Jamie," Beth said softly. "No one is going to hurt you. I can see how frightened you are. Can you tell me what is scaring you?"

As tears ran down my face, I whispered, "it feels like someone is touching me."

Beth continued to reassure me that I was safe. Eventually the real world came into focus and I realized where I was and with whom.

Beth was looking at me with a concerned look on her face. I looked down, embarrassed to find my arms wrapped tightly around my stuffed rabbit.

"What is wrong with me?" I asked, still trying to shake the feeling of being a small child.

Beth explained that I appeared to be having a body memory, which is when the body stores memories and remembers them through flashes of memory in your mind or through sensations. This can happen when the memories are too painful and the mind represses the memories to protect itself. I had already been told that the image of the hands that I was having earlier that week might be a flashback.

The toughest part about this body memory was realizing that I felt like a five or six year old child. "What the hell happened to me?" I asked myself, but I was terrified of the answer. I told Beth that I had always felt something was horribly wrong, but I couldn't remember what it was. Beth reassured me,

"When your mind is ready, you will remember what you need to in order to heal."

This was my first step in healing. Trusting Kathy and Beth enough to share my feelings, my fears and the terrible memories that threatened my sanity and my life. But as you stated in a previous letter, "three steps forward, one step back." That certainly applies here.

Sincerely,

Jamie

Letter 15 — Body And Mind Connection

Dear Jamie,

I am so glad that in the Psychotherapy Unit you met two kinds, caring and compassionate nurses who you could trust and open up. You were lucky to have them as your therapists. I have met many patients who met many doctors, nurses, psychiatrists, psychologists, social workers, and psychotherapists in their life, but never felt that connection that you felt with Kathy and Beth. I knew both of them when I worked at the hospital as they used to refer psychotherapy patients to me. It was also easier for you because they were women and motherly. It would have been harder for you if they were male therapists. Having therapy with female therapists also prepared you to have therapy with me, a male therapist.

Thanks for sharing your body memory that you shared with Beth. She provided you with such a safe environment that you could regress and recover your old memory.

Many people do not realize that our body is as mysterious as our mind. The question is that when the mind represses painful memories where do these memories go? Many therapists feel they go to the unconscious mind. There are some who feel that our bodies are part of our unconscious. Body and mind connection is a strange one. We see that more often in those emotional conditions that we call psycho-somatic conditions where mental tension affects the most vulnerable organ of the body: heart or skin or intestines.

Some therapists believe that repressed sexuality can create hysterical conversion reactions while repressed aggression can lead to psycho-somatic conditions.

Coming back to your experience of body memory. I agree with your therapist that when people feel safer and ready then the repressed memories start to surface. By going to a psychotherapy unit, you took the risk to get triggered but also a golden opportunity to heal and recover and get healthy. I am curious to know more about your healing journey in the psychotherapy unit.

Peacefully,

Dr. Sohail

Letter 16 — The Worst Was Yet To Come

Dear Dr. Sohail,

Looking back I realize just how unique and special the Psychotherapy program truly was. Patients lived on the ward twenty four hours a day, seven days a week with programs and individual sessions running five days a week. Even during evenings, nights and weekends, staff was always available to support the patients. And the level of care and concern the staff showed was always exemplary. It was this constant support and level of caring that made all the difference in my healing. I was very lucky to have Kathy and Beth as my therapists. Their kindness and compassion enabled me to open up and to trust them with devastatingly painful memories. Being with them on a daily basis not only made me feel safe, but kept me physically safe as well.

When I first started remembering the abuse, I would have fragmented flashbacks. Seeing what basically looked like a movie playing in my head freaked me out because I not only saw it but had all the feelings associated with it. Fortunately for me, I had Kathy and Beth to help me cope with the pain, fear and horror.

In a one to one session with Kathy, I was just sitting there and staring at the floor when suddenly the green carpet was lost as a foggy black and white video started playing before my eyes. Out of the fog emerged a big, black car driving down a gravel road. I can hear kids playing and see the school in the distance. The car stops and the passenger door opens. He is calling for me. Terror builds inside of me, but I can't scream. I shake my head. No please. No!

Kathy yells my name in an attempt to break through the memory. The sound of her voice comforts me. I want to run to her. Gradually, the present pulls me back and I see Kathy watching me with concern and caring.

"You're safe, Jamie," she reassured me. Her chair is pulled close to mine and she reaches out to hold my hand. The experience terrified me, but Kathy seemed unfazed.

I start to explain the video in my mind.

"Whose car was it?" she asks. Her voice filled with concern.

"My grandfather's," I reluctantly admit. I suggest that maybe my mind made it up because I had been thinking about him last night.

*"What did you feel when you saw the car?" Kathy asks.

"Intense fear."

"Why?" she probes.

As I try to rationalize that if my mind made it up then I have no reason to be afraid, the video in my mind starts to play again. When it ends, I find myself huddled in fear in the corner of the office with Kathy kneeling beside me, trying to reassure me that I am safe.

The flashbacks were very unnerving and left me feeling confused and lost, but Kathy and Beth kept reminding me that I was not alone. They reminded me that I was safe, and even kept a close watch over me to make sure I was safe from myself.

After several months in the program, I still felt suicidal at times. One night I wandered around the hospital grounds and ended up sitting on the porch of an abandoned unit. I read one of the poems that I wrote just after my recent suicide attempt.

Peace In The Sand

Feeling so bad all of the time

Think I'm going out of my mind,

I can't understand this pain I'm in

Wondering when did it begin,

And how did it ever get this far

Sharing The Secret

Now I stand again on the shore,

Watching my blood trickle onto the sand

God I don't understand,

Cut harder my mind screams

While the sun feverishly beams,

Down on me

God one last plea,

To make the cuts long and deep

So that I may find eternal sleep,

Too tired now to make a stand

God please try to understand

And let me find peace in the sand.

I still felt that way and now the desire to hurt myself was growing in its intensity. Luckily, I did not have anything sharp with me to use on my wrists so I just sat there. The feelings were strong but I didn't want to act on them

Dr. K Sohail and Jamie Lochlan

because if I did, I would get discharged immediately from the unit. This possibility scared the hell out of me. Without the unit, and Kathy and Beth, I knew that I would not survive on my own. I also did not want to give up my connection with Kathy and Beth. For the first time in my life, I felt understood and not so alone. I refused to give that up so instead of trying to figure out a way to hurt myself, I tried to find a way not to do it. Past experience had taught me that if I just held on and did not take action then the intense self-harm feelings would diminish. I decided to just hold on.

It was late when I finally returned to the unit. I went to the kitchen. *As I reached out to grab a butter knife from the drawer to make a sandwich, my hand started to shake. Suddenly I didn't trust myself to pick up a knife. Images of grabbing one of the sharper knives and thrusting it into my stomach or slashing it across my wrist bombarded my mind. I backed away from the drawer. Standing in the middle of the room, my eyes transfixed on the drawer, I didn't hear someone enter the kitchen.

"Jamie, are you okay?" the voice asked gently.

"Jamie," the voice called more insistently.

I shook my head and slowly turned to see Kathy standing behind me.

"You don't look okay," Kathy said as she tried to assess the situation.

"Can you tell me what's happening, Jamie?"

As I tried to speak and realized that I couldn't find the words, several people entered the kitchen. Feeling self-conscious and embarrassed, I bolted from the room with Kathy following closely behind.

"Jamie, let's go talk in the office okay," she said firmly but gently.

I stopped and followed her to the office.

"Can you tell me what's happening?" Kathy repeated after we both sat down.

Dr. K Sohail and Jamie Lochlan

I looked away and my face flushed with embarrassment as I realized how close I had been to grabbing the knife and hurting myself.

"Jamie, it's okay," Kathy encouraged me, "you can talk to me."

"Okay, I just have this overwhelming desire to slit my wrists right now," I chided as I shoved all of my emotions down and tried to chill my heart to not only the extreme pain, but also from the caring that I felt from Kathy.

"Is that's why you were staring so intently on the cutlery drawer in the kitchen?" Kathy asked.

I nodded and added sarcastically, "But I didn't think the knives would be sharp enough."

"You're right," Kathy said in a matter of fact tone. "We deliberately keep them dull, after all this is a psych hospital."

"Shit and I thought it was Club Med," I chimed in. "Remind me to fire my travel agent."

"So what's really going on?" Kathy asked as she looked at me intently and made eye contact.

Quickly, I directed my gaze to the floor but it was too late, her eyes had already met mine and I had seen the look of concern in them. Kathy really cares about you and you're being a complete asshole, I scolded myself.

"I'm sorry," I said softly. "I'm just a little overwhelmed."

"How strong are the suicidal feelings?" Kathy asked...

"Pretty strong."

"I know that you're really hurting now and you need all the support that you can get," Kathy said gently and then suggested that she call an emergency community meeting for me so that I could get extra support from the other patients.

"No way," I responded angrily. "No fucking way."

Kathy looked confused by my response and tried to explain that the purpose of the meeting was to help me.

"I don't want to be the center of attention," I explained. "I hate that."

I tried to tell Kathy that in the past whenever I became the center of attention it was either to get picked on verbally or physically, in either case I always got hurt.

"But if you're having very strong suicidal feelings, the community needs to know," Kathy explained.

Although I did not want to lose Kathy, it was preferable to being the focus of a community meeting so I decided to take a stand.

"If you call a meeting, I'll leave right now," I stated and then got up.

Realizing that I was serious and not playing a game, Kathy took a deep breath and asked me to wait.

"Can you control the suicidal impulses?" she asked.

"For now."

"If I agree not to call a meeting, will you promise me that you will tell me or another staff member if you feel that you are going to lose control," Kathy asked.

"I promise Kathy," I said softly and vowed to myself that I would keep my word.

Kathy smiled uneasily at me. I could see that she was second-guessing her decision.

"David and your parents would be devastated if you ever hurt yourself. And I would be devastated too," Kathy said so sincerely that I had to look away.

"I promise that I'll tell you."

As Kathy and I walked out of the office, she said that her shift was over and that my associate therapist Beth was on duty tonight if I needed to talk more. *

Even though I was hurting and overwhelmed with self-harm thoughts, I took comfort in knowing that Kathy cared and Beth did too. I knew that I could count on them to help because this was only the beginning of my remembering. The worst was yet to come.

Sincerely,

Jamie

Letter 17 — The Painful Truth

Dear Dr. Sohail,

The agony of not knowing who abused me and when often drove me to the edge of sanity. But with the support of Kathy and Beth I felt safe enough to remember the secret that I had buried since I was a young child.

I had been in the program for close to five months when a major flashback revealed the secret. On a weekend visit with my husband, he pulled me from behind to sit on his lap. He wanted to hug me. But my body didn't realize it was him and was triggered into releasing a major flashback. Describing that memory to Kathy was one of the most difficult things I have ever done. The horror was overwhelming. When I entered the room for our session, Kathy immediately knew that something was wrong and asked me what happened. Over our one-to-one sessions and spending social time together drinking tea and watching TV, I connected with Kathy and I felt closer to her and safer with her than

I had ever felt with anyone else before. I trusted her.

* "You're safe Jamie," she said in a mothering tone. "It's okay."

Here was the one woman that I cared for almost as much as my own mother, yet part of me wanted to run from her. The other part of me wanted to crawl into her arms and weep like a small innocent child.

"I saw me," I said and took a breath to finish the sentence. "I was little and in a car with a man."

I stopped and tried hard to keep breathing.

"You're safe, Jamie," Kathy said warmly. "Tell me what you saw."

"I was sitting on his lap," I whispered. "I was holding on to the steering wheel ...you know ... pretending to drive the car."

Then I stopped because it hurt to talk. I started to cry.

As tears streamed down my face, I gasped, "His pants were open. My little dress was pulled up."

I could not say any more. It hurt too much. Kathy reached over and put her hand on mine to comfort me. When I finally could speak, I asked her if I was going crazy.

Kathy smiled reassuringly, "No. You're not going crazy. I'm not sure yet, but it sounds like it might have been a flashback. With time, we'll know more."

"How old do you think you were?" Kathy asked.

"About five years old," I whispered.

"Did you recognize the man," Kathy continued.

I nodded slowly, almost painfully. Cold with fear, I crossed my arms across my chest and took a deep breath.

"It was my grandfather. I could not see his face, but it was his car, and his black jacket and pants. He used to pick me up after school and take me back to his place so my grandma could watch me until mom got off work."

"You said that his pants were open, can you tell me what he was doing?" Kathy asked very gently in the softest tone.

I started crying again at the image of me with my little red velvet dress lifted up at the back with the zipper part of his pants peering out from under my dress. My little hands were on the burgundy steering wheel. His big hands were around my ribs holding me down onto him.

I took a deep breath and whispered, "He was rubbing himself against me."

As I started shaking with pain and terror, Kathy moved closer to me and then asked if she could put her hand on my shoulder. I nodded. Her touch felt reassuring and kept me from completely losing myself in the pain and terror which soon turned to shock, rage and disgust. As I wondered how he could have hurt me, his little granddaughter, I was shocked not only by the realization of what he had done, but also that it had taken me almost two decades to remember it because I had buried the memory so deep. The feelings of betrayal gave way to blinding rage and a strong desire to kill the bastard who fortunately was already dead. Finally, feelings of disgust hit me with such force that I pulled away from Kathy's touch. I felt dirty. He had made me dirty.

"I feel so dirty," I cried.

"You're not," Kathy reassured me. "You were just an innocent child. He violated you. You have nothing to feel ashamed of."

"Why didn't I try to stop him?" I wondered aloud.

"Jamie, you were just a small child," Kathy stated. "You probably couldn't have stopped him even if you tried."

I felt so confused. Although I wanted to dismiss the horrific image as a product of my imagination, I knew in my heart that it was true. The image was so vivid and detailed. I could see the vibrant red velvet fabric of my dress, the burgundy steering wheel and dashboard, the little burgundy buttons on the seats, the blackness of his pants and jacket and those huge familiar hands holding me down onto him. This was the missing piece of my life. I had always felt that something was wrong in my life and now I knew what it was. Now I knew what I had been running from and that knowledge made me want to run even more.*

Something Isn't Right

Sometimes I think I'm losing my mind

Because I can't remember the time or place

Or even the face of the person

Who made my world so unsafe

Sharing The Secret

But I just have to look at my life

To know something isn't right.

All the time I feel this pain deep inside

Wearing me down until I want to die

I don't understand why to live I must fight

Something isn't right.

Sometimes my mind just isn't there

It's gone off alone and hidden somewhere

Other times I see pictures in my head

And I feel a child's fright.

No! Something isn't right.

Sometimes when my love tries to touch me in the night

I freeze in fear and beg him not to come near

Other times I wake with a scream on my lips

Because I've felt the touch of his fingertips

I can't explain my terror in the night

Dr. K Sohail and Jamie Lochlan

I just know something isn't right.

Then one night it all came to me

In a picture of my past reality

I saw me, young and small,

In a car with a man, and I saw it all

His pants were open and I was on his lap

Oh God, I didn't want to see that

But at least now when I'm scared in the night

I know what isn't right.

Sincerely,

Jamie

Letter 18 — Body Memories

Dear Dr. Sohail,

As bad as the flashbacks were that I had while in the Psychotherapy Program, the body memories were even worse. I was so confused by them and I couldn't even recognize what they were at first. The physical feelings that occurred for no known reason along with the intense emotional feelings were overwhelming and frightening. The memories that surfaced as a result were terrifying.

After I had the flashback of the incident in my grandfather's car, I was hit with an intense body memory.

* During the night, I woke with a scream upon my lips and a terrible soreness in my genital area. Suppressing the scream, I gasped for air as my mind reeled. *"Horsey"*. He called it horsey.

I limped out of the dorm and went down the hall to the bathroom. Clinging to the toilet, I heaved repeatedly until it was finally finished and I sat huddled on the floor, shaking. It was real. It was not part of my imagination. I actually remembered him calling it "horsey". I also once again felt all of the fear and anxiety that this word used to instill in me. I remembered that my private area used to hurt from him rubbing himself against me just as it did now with the body memory.

Suddenly I heard footsteps coming towards the bathroom. I wanted to jump up and shut the partially open door, but fear immobilized me. My mind was screaming that it was my grandfather coming to hurt me. The footsteps were at the door now, but soon faded. I breathed a sigh of relief. I stood up and opened the door fully. It squeaked. I poked my head out into the hall. No one was there. I turned to the sink and splashed some cold water on my face before going out into the hall. As I exited the bathroom, I bumped into someone. I jumped.

"Take it easy," the voice instructed.

I turned to see a petite brown-haired woman. It took me a few seconds to recognize Beth.

"Are you okay Jamie?" she asked with a puzzled look on her face.

I nodded and forced a smile. But Beth did not buy it. She motioned with her hand for me to go into the small meeting room. I flopped down onto the couch and started to cry.

"Beth, he called it 'horsey'. Fuck, it was my own grandfather," I cried.

Beth sat down beside me and gently put her hand on my shoulder. She reassured me that I was going to be okay. She told me that I survived the abuse as a child and that I would survive remembering the abuse as an adult. *

There were other body memories too. After I remembered that my grandfather abused me, I had a body memory that was extremely intense and I'm ashamed to admit it but I reacted violently.

My husband and I were sitting together on a couch and I playfully poked him in the cheek with a licorice stick. He told me to stop. But I suddenly felt like a playful little kid and poked him again. He grabbed the licorice stick out of my hand and said, "you eat it" as he tried to force it into my mouth. Overwhelmed with terror, I screamed for him to stop and started swinging my arms to protect myself. I hit him in the private area. He screamed. I didn't see my husband until his yelling brought me back to the present. I saw him cupping his genitals and looking at me in shock. He told me what I did. I was horrified that I hurt him.

When Beth tried to get me to tell her what happened, I was too ashamed.

* "It's okay Jamie. I've pretty much heard it all so there's nothing that you can say that will shock or disgust me. I just want to help you."

I looked up from the floor to see Beth smiling encouragingly at me. I told her about the licorice incident that had happened between David and me.

"How did you feel when he was trying to force the licorice into your mouth?" Beth asked.

"Terrified, like I was fighting for my life. I thought that he was going to hurt me really bad."

"You obviously did not realize that it was David," Beth stated, "or that it was just candy."

I shook my head indicating no, in agreement with Beth's statement. The person shoving something into my mouth was definitely not my husband.

"What was being forced into your mouth?" Beth questioned.

"I didn't know what it was at first," I said, my voice breaking with emotion. "I just thought that I had freaked out as usual. There was no explanation for it until now."

Beth leaned closer to me and smiled slightly to reassure me. She waited patiently for me to put into words a new horrible realization.

I took a deep breath. "Last night, I woke up from an awful dream. I was gagging and ran to the bathroom to throw up."

I stopped talking to try to control the nausea rising within me. Based on years of experience, Beth could have safely surmised what I was going to say, but she also knew that I needed to say what the dream had been about and confront it. In a very gentle tone, Beth asked me to tell her about the dream.

"I couldn't breathe. He was holding me so tight. I couldn't get away. He was trying to shove his penis in my mouth," I whispered as tears streamed down my face. "Then I saw myself in the dream at about age five or six and I'm crying uncontrollably."

I felt so ashamed that I wanted to run from the room, but instead curled up further into the couch and sobbed. Beth got up and sat down on the couch beside me. She put her hand on my shoulder.

"I know that you're going through a really rough time right now, but you're going to get through this, Jamie," she reassured me. "You survived the abuse; you'll survive remembering it too."

"I'm not so sure, Beth," I croaked. "I feel like I'm dying inside."

"He was my grandfather, Beth. My own grandfather," I cried. "How could he do that? I was just a kid."

"I'm so sorry that he hurt you," Beth said, trying to comfort me. "You're going to be okay Jamie." *

 After having a body memory or flashback, it is easy to get lost in my head and space out. Since being in the past hurts and being in the present hurts too, my mind takes off.

Unfortunately, I still have body memories sometimes. Not flashbacks as much. The body memories still throw me, but I can usually figure out what they are and understand what they are trying to tell me. I've learned to be patient and wait for the actual memory to come back after the body memory hits. They are still upsetting but I've learned to recognize them and deal with them. Even though it's difficult to talk about the body memories, I'm really glad that I can discuss them with you, Dr. Sohail.

Sincerely,

Jamie

Letter 19 — Writing About The Trauma

Dear Jamie,

I read your letters and felt sad, very sad. It is tragic that you were abused as a child and even worse that it was by a man you trusted. Rather than showering you with love and kindness he hurt you badly and made you suffer.

I can imagine that the experience of betrayal was so painful that your mind repressed it for so long. You were fortunate that finally you met two kind hearted, caring and compassionate therapists who offered you a safe environment to regress and retrieve those memories so that you can start the process of healing.

I am well aware that it is not easy even now to write about those traumatic experiences, but now you are at a higher stage of healing and recovering. It is a sign of growth that you can trust me, a male therapist, and share your past experiences of hurting and healing in writing. These letters will solidify your healing and also create a document that will offer hope to other young women, who were physically, emotionally and sexually abused as children, that they can also heal and recover, and create healthy and peaceful lifestyles for themselves and their dear ones. It will be your gift to suffering humanity.

Thank you for trusting me enough to share those encounters with therapy and healing.

Can you share how you were different when you left the Psychotherapy Unit as compared to when you entered it and what did you do after you were discharged?

Peacefully,

Dr. Sohail

Letter 20 — Therapeutic Relationships

Dear Jamie,

The more I reflect on your therapeutic relationship with Beth and Kathie, the more I realize that they were mature and experienced therapists who helped you work through some dark phases of your life. I have met many young and inexperienced therapists who dread working with patients with a history of physical, emotional and sexual abuse. They are preoccupied with saying the right words at the right moments in psychotherapy. Since they do not know what to say they feel embarrassed. I try to reassure them by saying that their caring, concern and compassion are more important than the right words they would like to utter. Their therapeutic relationship means more to their patients than their choice of words. In human relationships non-verbal communication is as important as verbal communication. As therapists we learn our style of caring. Each patient is unique and so is each therapist.

I share with my students that I learnt so much from my patients. They have been my teachers. They helped me become a more caring therapist and inspired me to become a more compassionate human being.

Peacefully,

Dr. Sohail

Letter 21 — Needing Hope

Dear Dr. Sohail,

When I entered the Psychotherapy Program, I felt depressed, desperate, alone, and confused about why I was in so much emotional pain that I wanted to end my life. I had no hope for my future. The one thing I needed more than anything was reassurance that I would be okay because in that reassurance I could find hope.

Once I started remembering the abuse, my therapists, Kathy and Beth, along with the other nurses on the unit were constantly reassuring me that I would be okay. I had a hard time believing them though because I was in so much emotional pain.

When I was trying to deny that the abuse happened, Kathy comforted me and I still hold on to her words.

*"It really did happen Jamie," Kathy consoled. "You just have to look at all the pain that you've felt in your life, the suicidal feelings, the hospitalizations, and the deep depression, to know that it's real, and that it hurt you. The abuse keeps hurting you. Jamie, if you don't face it and try to deal with it, it will continue to hurt you. You're a wonderful person. You deserve better. You can have a happier life."

"Do you really think so," I doubted.

"Yes, but it's going to take hard work for you to get there," Kathy explained.

Kathy smiled warmly. "Jamie, I can see you when you're hurting. I feel for you. I wish that I could take the pain away, but I can't. I know that you have to go through this and feel the pain in order to heal and be whole again. Healing is worth it. Think of the wonderful life that you and David could have. You just have to work through this to get past it. You will make it, Jamie. I know you will."

Kathy's words stirred something foreign within me; it was hope.* But she was always realistic and honest about how difficult the journey ahead of me would be.

When Kathy said that it would not be easy, but I would get through it and that I was going to be okay, I asked her, "Promise?" She replied, "Yes, I promise, but I also promise that it will hurt at times too." And she wasn't kidding.

In one of the psychodrama groups, I got triggered by a woman screaming and one of the nurses, Ann, tried to comfort me.

I was shaking and crying. I buried my head in my arms and prayed for the screaming to stop.

*Realizing that I had been triggered by the fear release, Ann tried to get my attention by calling my name. She dared not touch me in case her touch threw me into a deeper state of terror. Ann knelt down in front of me and tried to make eye contact. She continued to call my name and tell me that I was safe.

Finally after several minutes, Ann broke through to me. Trembling and still sobbing, I tried to tell Ann about the flashback and how terrified I was of my grandfather. Ann led me out of the room so that we could talk privately while Sonya and the rest of the group continued the fear release. Once in the hall, Ann and I talked for a long time about the flashback and how devastated I was by the possibility that I may have been raped.

"Trust your gut feeling Jamie," Ann told me. "It knows your truth. Your mind will too when you're ready to remember."

"Remembering is hard enough," I stated. "I don't think that I will ever get over the abuse."

"You will in time," Ann said with a smile, "if you're willing to work really hard."

"Sure," I said sarcastically as I wondered how much therapy work would ever be enough to alleviate the damage done by the abuse. Inside I felt as if I had been broken beyond any hope of repair. . .

Ann looked me straight in the eye and said, "You will get over this Jamie. Do you know how I know that?"

I shrugged my shoulders and continued looking at her curiously.

"Because I see it everyday. I see the women in the psychodrama groups get stronger. They move out of their shame and fear into their anger. They grow emotionally and start to heal," Ann said her voice filled with confidence. "Gradually, they heal to the point where the abuse does not affect their daily life."

"Do you mean that someone can actually get over this and have a real life?" I questioned with a surprised look on my face.

"Yes, if you work really hard, you can get over this Jamie," Ann said and offered me a hug.

Grateful for the hug, I smiled at Ann, but I was even more grateful for the gift of hope.*

Beth was constantly reassuring me. She would often tell me that she was sorry that my grandfather hurt me and that I would be okay. Every session ended with her reminding me that I would be okay.

The one thing I needed more than anything to survive remembering the abuse was hope. Hope that I would be okay. And unfortunately, hope was something that I had not felt in a very long time. It was a wonderful gift that my therapists gave me. I also needed someone to care. The caring that I received from Kathy and Beth made all of the difference in the world. I never doubted that they cared for me. I would not have survived if it wasn't for them and the Psychotherapy Program.

When I left the Psychotherapy Program, I felt lost. Going from having support seven days a week, twenty four hours a day to only a one hour a week session for follow up until I found a permanent therapist was terrifying and isolating. Even when I found a permanent therapist, one hour a week was not enough. My depression got worse. I couldn't discuss my feelings or memories with my spouse so I was very much alone.

Unable to cope with the isolation, I joined an A.M.A.C. (Adults Molested As Children) group and another group for sexual assault survivors. It might have seemed like overkill to my spouse, but it kept me out of the hospital and enabled me to function. I attended the weekly groups for a few years until I felt confident enough to just have weekly one to-one sessions with a private therapist for support.

Sincerely,

Jamie

Letter 22 — Gift Of Hope

Dear Jamie,

I am so glad that you recognized that your therapists offered you a gift of hope. When people are feeling helpless, powerless and hopeless, a gift of hope is very special and precious. But it is also important that the hope offered is realistic and authentic because false hope can easily backfire.

The Psychotherapy Program offered a valuable service to patients who struggled with childhood abuse. There was one problem though. The Psychotherapy Program did not have an aftercare program for their discharged patients.

Discharged patients belonged to two groups.

The first group had successfully completed their program and were discharged after their graduation. They were healed and were stable.

The second group had broken the rules and were thrown out of the program. They were generally raw and angry and unstable. I called them therapeutic miscarriages.

Over the years I had helped both groups and offered them support and stability in the outpatient department. Psychotherapy staff were very appreciative of the follow up I provided to their discharged patients.

A few years later Psychotherapy staff also created a program in the community called Beacon House. That program offered help to people living in the community. I am not sure what happened to the Psychotherapy Unit and Beacon House. I think both programs closed down.

Peacefully,

Dr. Sohail

Letter 23 — The Betrayal

Dear. Dr. Sohail,

Trust. Such a simple word but so powerful! When trust has been destroyed at such a young age, the affects are long lasting. I have always had trouble trusting people with my feelings and even with my personal safety and that of those I love, as a result of the abuse by a trusted adult when I was a young child. There have been people in my life that I am very glad that I let in and trusted them, but there have been others that abused that trust even though they knew the price I would pay for the betrayal.

About three years ago, my son's bandmate, I'll call him A, joined his band and started staying over at our house since he lived in another city. He seemed nice and tried hard to fit in with the family. He even started calling me Mom. The more I got to know A, the more I realized that he desperately wanted to belong in a family. We treated him like family. If he needed clothes, shoes, gas money, we helped out as much as we could, and supported and encouraged his musical aspirations. He repaid us by lying to us on a regular basis about everything and anything. Turns out he is a compulsive liar. He also stole from us. When he cheated on his fiance and she ended the relationship, she started asking us about items that we supposedly gave to A. That's how we found out he had been stealing from us for three years. My son and I were devastated and furious. We had trusted him and treated him like family. A was fired from the band for theft. Things went from bad to worse when A started asking our friends for money and tarnished my son's reputation as a result. Three months after we fired him, we are still doing damage control with respect to my son's career. My too kind-hearted son was actually considering asking A back if he turned his life around, stopped lying and stealing. Unfortunately, A again went too far and took advantage of someone close to us. Now my son will never let him back in the band. I can't say that I'm surprised by A's actions; just very disappointed in him. He manipulates people so that he can use and take advantage of them. He certainly did that with me and my son. He has no regard for the people that have tried in good faith to help him and been very supportive of him. He uses their caring and concern like a weapon against them. He doesn't take any responsibility for his actions and cannot see how he betrayed us and ruined our trust. A hard lesson learned; I will never be that welcoming to a stranger again. My guard is permanently up.

Sincerely,

Jamie

Letter 24 — Painful Experience

Dear Jamie,

I really feel bad that you had such a traumatic experience especially with someone you treated like your son. He did not realize that you had provided him with a second family, from an emotional as well as creative point of view. I am sure one day he will regret it. Life will teach him a few lessons, some of them not so pleasant. I have met many writers and actors and artists who were delinquents. They were talented artists but did not have a sense of ethics. They did not want to follow any rules. They did not realize that for them to be successful writers and artists they need to work on their personalities alongside their art. There are many male and female artists who abuse alcohol and drugs and sex. In the beginning they think it is fun but with passage of time they realize that their fans do not respect them and finally leave them because they feel betrayed the way you felt betrayed. Trust is important not only in personal but also in professional and artistic relationships.

Dear Jamie,

In spite of this painful experience I do not want you to feel discouraged. You did not do anything wrong, he was the one who wronged you and took advantage of your good nature. You are caring and nurturing and motherly so you treated him like your son. That is your strong point. I do not want you to feel guilty or embarrassed about it.

You are such a wonderful loving mother. You trust your children and they trust you.

I am curious at what stage of your life you decided to become a mother and how did your mothering experience change your personality and lifestyle?

Peacefully,

Dr. Sohail

Letter 25 — Deciding To Become A Mother

Dear Dr. Sohail,

When I was twenty eight years old, my husband and I went to visit my cousin who had just had her first child. As I held her beautiful three-day old infant, I knew in my heart that I wanted more than anything to have my own baby. My husband and I had previously discussed having children and although he felt ready, I wasn't at the time. But now I knew I was ready to consider it. After having done group and individual therapy for about two years after leaving the Psychotherapy Program, I realized that most of my life had been about the abuse and that I had lost my childhood, my teen years and most of my twenties to my abuser. I didn't want my life to be about just surviving the abuse. I wanted to live and not give my abuser one more day of my life. I asked myself what do I want my life to be about? What do I want for myself? The answer: I want to be a mother. Holding that beautiful baby brought everything into focus for me.

I realized that being a mother would be life changing for me. Being realistic, I knew that having a child would not "fix" me and make the depression disappear. I understood that depression was probably something I would have to deal with for the rest of my life because of the abuse. But I could deal with the depression and still have a life that was mine. But I could not bring a child into the world if I had any intention of deliberately leaving them. They deserved to have a mother who would be there to raise them and love them. I had to promise myself and my future children that suicide would never be an option, no matter how bad the depression got. And I had to promise myself to reach out for help when I needed it and to continue with therapy if I needed it, so that I could be the best mother that I could possibly be. I made that promise and before my 30th birthday, my first child was born. My precious baby girl J.

The birth of my daughter made me value life in a way that I never had before. I valued the life of my precious baby but I also started to value my own life, for her sake. My focus was no longer on myself but on her. I got swept up in motherhood. My life revolved around fulfilling her needs: feedings, diaper changes, baths, naps, bedtime, and the never ending laundry. And even though it was difficult and exhausting, I loved my new role as her mom. The sweetest thing was rocking J to sleep in the middle of the night, and then holding her and watching her sleep in my arms. For the first time in a very long time, I was happy. Two and a half years later my precious son Q was born, and our family was complete. My husband and I were happy. My life felt full and meaningful, and had purpose. I felt I mattered, especially to my beautiful babies. I love being their mom! Raising J and Q, and watching them grow up has been both my greatest accomplishment and my greatest joy! I'm so incredibly proud of them! They taught me how to be compassionate, kind and to love on a deeper level that I never understood before.

Sincerely,

Jamie

Letter 26 — Breakthrough

Dear Jamie,

Deciding to become a mother was a turning point in your life.

On one hand it helped you take responsibility for your own life and make healthy choices about your future and on the other hand you became more nurturing to your children. You had to rise above your problems to take care of them. I find it interesting that your deciding to become a mother coincided with your decision to not commit suicide.

To me it seems that at that crossroads you chose life over death, health over sickness, happiness over suffering.

It was like a breakthrough in your life.

Your experience of mothering was such a delightful adventure for you. You are one of the most caring and loving mothers I have met in my life. When you talk about your children your face lights up. Recently I have seen the same excitement in your voice when you talk about your dog. I sometimes wonder whether your dog has become your third child, especially knowing that your children are grown up and planning to leave the home in the next couple of years. Your dog might be the only child left behind.

Now I want to know how you found out about our Creative Psychotherapy Clinic and how therapy in our clinic was similar or different from the therapy you received before.

You have been coming regularly to our clinic for a number of years. What does therapy with me mean to you?

Peacefully,

Dr. Sohail

Letter 27 — Starting Therapy With Dr. Sohail

Dear Dr. Sohail,

Thank you for saying that I am one of the most caring and loving mothers that you have met. It really means a lot to me. Being a mother is the most important thing in my life. My kids are everything to me.

And you are correct that my beautiful puppy Charlie is my third child. Both my husband and I dote on her and cherish her. She brings a lot of love and happiness into our home. My kids love her dearly too. We got Charlie almost three years ago, after the death of our fourteen year old Chihuahua. We were all devastated to lose her. When we got Charlie, she was just a little four pound, eight week old puppy. Although we all missed our old dog and mourned her passing, Charlie helped us to heal.

Dear Dr. Sohail,

I found out about your clinic from my family doctor when J was about two years old and I was pregnant with my second child. I met with you only a few times before having to suspend sessions due to difficulties with my pregnancy. Then once my son was born, I was too busy to resume therapy. When J was five years old and Q had just turned two years old and started nursery school, I was struggling with depression again along with the demands of raising young children. I was also dealing with new memories of the abuse, which were violent and terrifying for me. The memories made me feel confused, angry and in a lot of emotional pain. I was afraid of losing control. Knowing that my children needed me and always honoring the promise I made before they were born to never act on suicidal feelings, I called your office and told your receptionist Ann that I needed to start therapy again for my kids' sake and mine.

When I first started regular sessions with you, I was guarded and only discussed easy topics like my children or motherhood. I steered away from the real reason I was there; the deep emotional pain resulting from the memories of the abuse and the pull towards suicide that I still felt. Although I had worked with a few male therapists at the Psychotherapy Program, I had never really opened up to them, and was always guarded and reluctant to trust a male since my abuser had been a man. You must have realized my struggle, since you never pushed me to open up. Instead you told me that you were a writer too and you encouraged me to write and share those writings with you. Alone is one of the poems that I wrote during that time.

Alone

I saw your smile

And it touched my soul.

Now I'm struggling to remember

How to hold it all together

Because I can't feel your love.

And you won't give me a smile

To light my darks ways

To help push away the demons

Of yesterday and today.

Alone

Just needing a friend

Not the one dragging me

To the bloody end.

I keep fighting

For the babies in my arms

And the love I had in you.

But I'm still standing here.

Alone

Screaming for you to see

Sharing The Secret

The girl in the woman

Needing to be loved.

Alone

I thought I was happy

But that was never true

Because I still can't find you.

Alone.

You also encouraged me to write about my experiences in the Psychotherapy Unit. The result was my novel *"SHORE OF NOWHERE"*. I've included excerpts (marked with an asterisk *) from it in these letters. Every week I would read the newest chapter to you. We didn't discuss it afterward. At the time I didn't understand why because the other female therapists that I worked with would have done that. Now I understand why; if you had pushed me to discuss those painful experiences then I would have put my walls up and shut down because the trust was not there since I was not able to trust a male therapist yet. By writing about my experiences and reading those writings to you, you were able to learn about my past and about the abuse in a way that was not threatening for me. You were also connecting with me, writer to writer, which built the trust that was needed. Looking back, I realize and appreciate how you built that trust between us.

Now I feel that I can tell you anything. The trust is there. The minute I walk into your office, I feel my walls drop. During our weekly sessions, it's the only time that I feel safe, accepted and understood. I know that you care and feel your concern, and as a result I feel safe discussing with you the most painful memories of the abuse, the depression and my daily struggles. Outside of our sessions, I am alone in dealing with the abuse and my depression. I can't discuss these issues with my husband, or anyone else. A lot of what I went through is too horrific for an untrained person to handle. It's too much for any spouse or friend. I know that. Sessions with you are my life-line. I know that I would not survive on my own. The depression, the memories of the abuse, and the Obsessive Compulsive Disorder would overwhelm me. Our sessions are my safety net, my safe place. I know that I can count on you to help me and if necessary, to protect me from myself if I ever feel out of control and suicidal. I just have to reach out to you and tell you.

Sincerely,

Jamie

Letter 28 — Pandemic

Dear Dr. Sohail,

Well along with 7.64 billion other people, I can't believe we are living through a global pandemic. It's hard to wrap my brain around it. I see the death toll climbing daily and my heart breaks. Every day is filled with worry about the health and safety of my loved ones. And the nights are worse when the fear creeps in with the darkness. I feel powerless to protect my family, to fight an invisible foe, and to hope. Depression wraps itself around me like a weighted blanket that I can't free myself from. My sleep is restless and when I awake in the morning, for a brief moment I think that it's all been just a horrible nightmare, and then I realize it's real and I want to crawl back into bed and hide under the covers. I force myself to focus on each hour as it passes and not think about a bigger picture. This helps a lot to get through the day. My dog Charlie is a huge comfort, especially now. She always makes me smile even when I feel like I want to curl up in a ball and cry.

The wanting to cry part is happening more frequently lately. I feel sad, scared, overwhelmed and very depressed. I feel like I have no control over my life. I just want to be held and told that everything will be okay. I wish my husband could do that for me, but he won't and I won't ask. He minimizes my feelings so I'm left alone with them. Writing is my only outlet. And listening to music. Damnit Adele's song Remedy is going to make me cry. Most of the time I can keep a lock on my feelings, but today is not one of them. Just wrote this poem now. Not even sure what it means.

Fall

In a field,

Dried and brown

Life has not gone on.

Dr. K Sohail and Jamie Lochlan

I'm standing on the graves

Of hopes and Dreams

Love was never free

I've always paid

The steepest of prices

Roll the dices

I always come up empty

A lost soul

In a burning home

The flames kiss my face

Tears have left their trace

The world is spinning

Out of control

I can't grab hold

Slipping between my fingers

Like grains of sand

Sharing The Secret

All that I am

Fall ...

From past experience, I know these feelings will pass, maybe not tomorrow or the next day, but they will eventually pass and I will feel better. In the meantime, I just have to be kind to myself and allow myself to have my feelings. As a child I couldn't express my feelings about the abuse or even acknowledge them so I buried my feelings along with the memories. Now I allow myself to feel, even if it hurts. And sometimes it hurts a lot.

But as much as it hurts, I remind myself that I am capable of feeling joy too. And I can have hope. Hope is the one thing that has carried me through the darkest of times and it will carry me through again. Sometimes I have to look really hard to find hope, but I always find it. I find both hope and joy in my children, especially when it feels like the world is spinning out of control. I hold on to my children and hope for the world to become safe again for them.

Sincerely,

Jamie

Letter 29 — Writing Therapy

Dear Jamie,

You have far better recollections of our earlier therapy sessions than I have. For me some memories are vague and foggy. I remember encouraging you to write and you sharing your creations in your sessions with me. I was always impressed by what you wrote and how you wrote. I remember you struggling with the idea of writing with a pseudonym. You were in a conflict. You wanted to share your story with the world but you were unsure whether you could do it with your real name. You did not want to hurt or offend any of your relatives. So I let you write and figure out your feelings as a survivor of abuse and also as a writer.

With the passage of time you gained more confidence as a woman as well as a writer. And now writing these letters as a part of the book, *Sharing the Secret*, I see a more confident person who is ready to share her secret with the world and offer hope to other young girls and women. I am confident your story will inspire them to transform their breakdowns into breakthroughs. I am so proud of you.

 Now I want to ask you how your father's death affected you, how you found out that you had a brother and how meeting him in person affected you emotionally because those experiences had a significant effect on your life.

Peacefully,

Sohail

Letter 30 — Death And Secrets

Dear Dr. Sohail,

Sorry for the late reply. These past two weeks have been very hectic and stressful. My husband and I bought a new build-house last June and we just received notice that it will be ready for occupancy this September so we have been busy packing and getting our existing house ready to sell. Trying to sell under normal circumstances is taxing, but during a global pandemic takes this stress and anxiety to a whole new level. Although I've been losing sleep worrying, I try to remind myself "This too shall pass" and try to stay positive that everything will work out fine.

To answer your question Dr. Sohail, my Dad and I always had a complicated relationship. I always felt that he never really knew or understood me, nor did I really know or understand him. We had always given each other a wide berth. My father never tried to build a relationship with me and never let me get close. He always deferred to my mother when it came to me so we never really had our own relationship. It often seemed that it was my mom and me, and then there was Dad. He was just there; the guy who was either working at the steel plant or out doing God-knows what, or if he was home, he was working in his garage, sleeping or demanding dinner. In the winters, he often took my cousins and me skiing, but would rarely spend time with us once we had learned how to ski. In the summers, he would swim with us in the family pool. But over all he liked to do his own thing, separate from his family and without the constraints of a family. He didn't even want to pick me up from school or take care of me when I was sick and couldn't go to school and my mother had to work.

I didn't realize until I was an adult that my father had positioned himself almost as an outsider in our family. He was always half-in, and half out. He told my mother once that "he was all fucked up" when she confronted him about his many affairs that threatened to rip our family apart. As an infant and toddler, I had naturally been oblivious to my parents' marital problems and didn't even find out until I was an adult that we had often lived with my mother's parents when my father had abandoned us to pursue another one of his affairs. As an older child around ten years old, I became aware of my parents' marital problems and the volatile nature of their relationship. My father when confronted or angered would simply leave. As a result, both my mother and I learned to avoid confrontation or do anything to make him angry for fear that he would leave. We walked on eggshells. Every few years my father would have an affair and threaten to leave our family so I never really knew from one day to the next if he would be around. As a result, I grew up learning that my mother was the only one I could count on. And I kept my father at a distance. It wasn't until my father became a grandfather that he started to be a real father.

When my first child J was born, my Dad was overjoyed. He absolutely adored J and would help take care of her and play with her. He loved being a grandfather. And when my son Q was born, he was ecstatic. He loved his grandkids and enjoyed spending time with them, telling them stories and taking them "Monster Hunting" a game he made up just for them. At times I would see my father watching my husband with the kids, and I could see in my Dad's eyes the realization of what he had missed with me and the regret. He became a better father to me and started to spend time with me and took me for coffee and breakfast. We started to build our own relationship. And to be honest, I loved my Dad, and I also liked him as a person and enjoyed spending time with him. I admired his intelligence and his ability to fix or make anything he desired whether it was to build a house, do home renovations, rebuild and fix a car or make a wooden chair for his grandchild.

Just before my 38th birthday, my Dad passed away suddenly at the age of sixty one. A few months before he died, I learned that I was not the only one with a secret. My Dad had been hiding the truth from me my whole life; that he had another child.

Just before the last Christmas that I would spend with both of my parents, I was shopping with my Mom in Walmart getting gifts for the kids and we stopped at McDonalds for lunch. She started talking about my father's history of affairs to which I replied, "Considering how many affairs he had, I'm surprised that I don't have a sibling or two out there somewhere." My mother replied, "I think you do and his name is Joshua". I dropped my Big Mac.

It turns out that his name wasn't Joshua. I never got the chance to confront my Dad about him. My Dad got sick with what we thought was the flu, but he died from Severe Coronary Artery Disease.

My Dad's death threw me and my family into a tailspin. We were all in shock for several months. For two to three years I just went through the motions. I barely remember those years. It was all I could do to cope with raising young children and survive. I wrote "STUMBLE AND FALL" for my Dad.

Stumble And Fall

My heart quickens

At the path before me

As fog fills my mind

Where do I turn this time?

I look behind

But you're not there

I miss the way

You used to care

With four words

You could ease my fears

You made the path

Seem so clear

But sadly you're not here.

Sharing The Secret

You've gone where one day

I will follow.

But now the road is mine alone

To travel.

I often stumble and fall

Making a mess of it all.

And rarely do I know the way

But mostly I just need you to say

It will be okay.

Although it's been fifteen years since my Dad passed away, I think about him every day and still really miss him. He left a giant hole in all of our lives. I often talk to my kids about him so that they can remember him and tell them that their Pa (grandfather) loved them and is proud of them. I'll always regret that I never got the chance to ask my Dad about my half-brother and why he never told me about him. But I am grateful that my

Dad and I were in a good place when he did pass and that he knew that I love him.

Dr. Sohail, since this was such a long letter, I'll save the discourse on my half-brother for the next letter.

Sincerely,

Jamie

Letter 31 — Skeletons In the Closet

Dear Jamie,

I felt sad reading that your father was an outsider and you did not get all the love and affection you needed and deserved as the only daughter. I think you were triangulated between your parents' conflicts. Your father wanted to avoid your mother so he also avoided you.

I felt glad reading that he became a better grandfather than a father and you were able to spend some special time with him before he died. At least you have some fond memories of his last few years on earth.

Your family, like many other families, had a few skeletons in the closet and one of them was your brother. Your father did not have the courage to discuss that with you. I think he must have been worried about what that might do to your mother. He wanted to avoid any conflict to keep peace. In some dysfunctional families, what seems like peace is actually a euphemism for a cold war.

I am glad that you survived all that and there was a light at the end of the tunnel for you. You were able to have a better relationship with your children than you had with your father as a child. Some parents teach us what to do in life and some teach us what not to do in life.

Now I am looking forward to reading the details about your relationship with your brother. How did you find him? How was your first meeting with him? How did the relationship evolve? And how is that relationship now?

Peacefully,

Dr. Sohail

Letter 32 — My Father's Son

Dear Dr. Sohail,

My husband and I finally got the house listed and up for sale. Now the waiting for a buyer begins. Our stress levels are through the roof. But I'm trying to remain positive and focus on my mental health. I know how quickly I can slide into a deep depression so I've learned to watch for my warning signs like losing interest in things, feeling angry and frustrated, feeling hopeless, feeling alone and feeling like I don't matter. All of these rising emotions signal that I'm falling into depression so to counteract them; I try to make sure I get enough sleep because lack of sleep triggers my mood becoming unstable. I also try to give myself a "Me Day" and just do whatever I feel like, such as watch TV or read or play with my dog Charlie. Giving myself permission to take time for myself reinforces that I matter to me and that I have value to me. It really helps. I also try to find joy in the simple things like giving my kids or my dog a hug, or watching my dog play with a favorite toy. Just little things that bring a smile to my face. I also try not to dwell too much on my past. I've learned the importance of letting go. It was a hard lesson.

Letting go of my hopes for my relationship with my half-brother was very difficult and painful. When I found out about him, I searched social media, the internet and even hired a private investigator to find him. Since my mom knew very little about him except for his mother's name and that he was born when I was three years old, I tried to go straight to the source. But his mother ignored my letters and all of my attempts to contact her. She obviously knew who I was and what I wanted. She wasn't having any of it. For about five years, I kept running into dead ends. But I didn't give up hope. I found out what university he had attended and that he had gone to the same high school as my husband. One night, my husband was on LinkedIn and on a whim he searched my brother's name and found him and where he worked.

Concerned that my brother would ignore me the way his mother did, I decided to show up at the office where he worked. On January 29th 2010, I went to his office, gave the receptionist my name and told her who I was waiting for. I was so nervous I thought I was going to throw up. The minute he walked out of the elevator, I knew it was him; he looked like a younger version of my Dad. I told him who I was looking for and asked him if he knew who I was. He smiled and said, "Yes you're my sister." He said that his mother told him about me after our father's death and that he had wanted to look for me. We went to a coffee shop to talk more privately. He showed me photos of his wife who was pregnant with their second child and their three year old daughter. I was ecstatic. I had a niece. He said we would get together and get to know each other and our families. He said that we had the same colour eyes and joked that he was taller than me.

We exchanged a few emails, then on May 5th 2010, just after my 43rd birthday, I got a phone call from him. He told me that he did not have any time for me in his life, that he did not want a sister and asked me to never contact him again. I told him that he would never hear from me again. I was devastated. I understood that for my brother our father was a difficult and painful topic and me by proxy, but I had hoped that we could get past that since we both had been victims of our father and his mother's decisions.

Although I didn't agree with his decision, I respected his request and kept my word and did not contact him. For three years I didn't hear from him, then in July of 2013 just as my family and I were about to catch a flight to Italy for a family trip, I got a phone call from him. His youngest daughter who was now three years old was very sick with leukemia. My heart broke. I just wanted to help him and my little niece any way that I could. My brother wanted to know the family's health history. I gave him all the information that I could and even my mother helped fill in details. My brother said he would stay in touch. I told him I would pray for his baby girl and to let me know if I could do anything to help them. I lit a candle and said a prayer for my little niece in every church that I went into in Italy.

When we returned from vacation, my brother and I stayed in touch by email. That continued for about three years. When his youngest daughter was about six years old and his oldest was about nine years old, my daughter J and I got to meet them for the first time at a restaurant for lunch. My little nieces were so adorable and so smart. I couldn't wait to spoil them, get to know them and be the best aunt to them. Then a few months after that my brother and his family came to my house for a visit where they got to meet my son Q. My husband was unfortunately away on a trip at the time. It was an incredible day! A day that I had hoped for, for a long time.

That was the last time I saw them. My brother stopped responding to my emails and text messages, and requests to meet. After nine years of this erratic relationship, I texted him on July 17th 2019 for the last time.

"Hi I just wanted to tell you that I only wish all the best for you and your family. When I found out about you, I searched for years and even hired a private investigator. I was so happy when I found you. I had truly hoped that we could get to know each other and be in each other's lives, maybe be siblings or at the least friends, but we are barely acquaintances. Your lack of response and ignoring my requests to meet make it clear that you are not interested in building a relationship. I'm not going to ask any more. It hurts to hope for something that will never happen. I'm not angry about how things have turned out. Just disappointed and sad. If I've got this all wrong then tell me. Otherwise, you won't be hearing from me any more. Take care little brother. Goodbye "

I received his reply that same day.

"I'm sorry to have hurt you. You have a very nice family, and it was good to meet all of you, but I don't want to lead you on. It's hard to convey how privately I prefer to live my life. In recent years, I find myself selfishly

Sharing The Secret

backing away from relationships to save myself for as much precious time with my young family as work life will allow. I wish you all the best."

The door that I had opened nine years ago was now closed. It really hurt to know that I did not matter to him; when he mattered so much to me. I was very disappointed, hurt and sad that I would never get to know my brother or his family. But I knew in my heart that the door had already been shut by him a long time ago. He just didn't tell me. I was now able to stop hoping for something that would never happen. I channeled my feelings into a new poem.

Cradle To Grave

It's over

Lost and gone.

The Dream I had

Of us

Cannot go on.

No hugs or hellos

Come my way.

You've forgotten my name.

We should have shared

From cradle to grave.

But when I found you

You turned away.

I had hoped for

So much more,

A brother and friend

Worth fighting for.

But I can't carry

What doesn't exist.

From your shadow

I need to walk away

Sharing The Secret

There is no tomorrow

And never was a yesterday.

Nothing ever said

Can make this okay.

I will always regret how things turned out with him. I had hoped for so much more and am left with only regrets: I will never know my brother and my nieces, and my children will never know their uncle and cousins. I had hoped for a brother and friend, and uncle for my children, but he obviously didn't want that. We will always be strangers. And that makes me very sad.

Sincerely,

Jamie

Letter 33 — A Mystery

Dear Jamie,

It is a sad, very sad story. I remember the times when you were looking for your brother everywhere.

I remember the day when you were ecstatic that you found his whereabouts.

I also remember the day you physically met him in Toronto. You were on cloud nine. But there was something about the whole encounter that made me uncomfortable. In the back of my mind I wondered what his mother had told him about your father and you, especially knowing that she never responded to your letters. I wondered whether his mother would let him develop a friendship with you. But then his mother died and I felt relieved. I thought the last obstacle was over. I was optimistic that both of you would spend a lot of time together and both of you would meet each other's family and then have regular family meetings.

But that never happened. He stepped back. It is still a mystery for me why he did that. I would have understood if after the first meeting with you he stated that he had a busy life and had no time to engage with a new family. But he did not. He even introduced you to his children and then met your children. After that meeting why he walked away, I am still puzzled. We might never know the real reason but you have to accept it to be at peace with yourself.

I hope you realize that you did everything possible to have a brother in your life. Your conscience is clear. Unfortunately he never fully reciprocated your feelings. I still feel there is more to the story that he did not share with you and he might take that part of the story to his grave.

Now I am interested in your relationship with your mother and how it changed after your father's death. How do you feel knowing that she lives alone with her dog, especially during the Corona Virus Crisis? What will you do if she is unable to take care of herself? Would you bring her to live with your family or admit her to a long term care for the elderly? Do you worry about your mother's health and happiness?

I hope your house sells quickly and you get the money you are asking for.

Peacefully,

Dr. Sohail

Letter 34 — My Mom

Dear Dr. Sohail,

When I found out that my father had died, my only thought was, " I've got to get to Mom." The thought that she was alone and dealing with his sudden death, made me feel anxious and panicky. My husband, the kids and I drove North through a snowstorm to try to get to her, but we ended up having to stay at a hotel that night because the roads were not safe because of the storm. I didn't steep all night, worrying about Mom.

When we finally got there, my focus was helping Mom. It's a blur now, but I remember seeing my Dad's body at the hospital and saying goodbye to him. Then the focus was on making arrangements for a memorial service and helping Mom with insurance and lawyers. We just tried to focus on the necessary tasks and buried our emotions.I had to be strong for her and my kids. It took several years to deal with my Dad's sudden passing. My Mom and I were both just going through the motions. His death had torn a hole in both of our lives and we were never the same.

Since my Dad's passing, I feel more protective of Mom than ever and my sense of responsibility for her increased, but initially, I also felt frustrated. I had just found out about my half-brother and was frustrated and angry that both my parents had hid his existence from me. My mother had only recently told me about him and my father died before I could confront him about it. I eventually came to the conclusion that it was my father's responsibility to tell me, not my mother's, and that I shouldn't blame her for my father's deceit.

In the midst of it all, I wondered if I should ask my Mom to move in with us. I realized that my father had asked his mother to move in with him after his dad died, and my grandmother lived with us until her death at the age of sixty eight. She never remarried even though she was widowed at thirty eight. Her life revolved around her family and work. I felt that my Mom was still young enough at fifty nine years old to have a life after her husband's death. I didn't want her to be alone. I had hoped that she would build a life for herself and find another partner to share her life with, or at least try. So I came to the conclusion that if I asked her to move in with us, then she would never build her own life or try finding a partner. I only wanted the best for her, and to be honest, I didn't think her living with us would be best for her. So instead I invited her to stay with us for 6 weeks or as long as she wanted after she settled Dad's affairs. Ever since that initial visit, Mom stays with us every year for four to six weeks. And until a few years ago when both kids started working in the summer, I used to take the kids and stay with her for a month every summer as well. I look forward to her visits and cherish the time that we spend together. I'm so proud of the strong, independent woman that she has become.

But I still worry about my Mom a lot. I hate that she and her dog are alone. I feel guilty that she is not here with me. She was supposed to come for a visit on her birthday in April, but because of Covid-19 her flight was cancelled in March. I thought about driving to her town to pick her and her dog up, but the reality is that my household is not safe for her; it is too busy with my kids going out to work and having the occasional friend visit. I cannot keep her safe here. And all I really want is for her to be safe, along with my kids and husband. If she needs me, I won't hesitate for a second to drive there to be with her.

A child often takes a mother's love for granted. It wasn't until I held J for the first time that I realized just how much my own mother loves me and this realization changed our relationship for the better. It also made me realize how much my mother values my life and I deeply regret all the pain I caused her when I was suicidal. I realize now that even though I went through some very dark times, she did too. We have found common ground. I cherish her, and always try to be patient and loving with her.

Sincerely,

Jamie

Letter 35 — New Nest, Empty Nest, Safety Nest

Dear Dr. Sohail,

The past few months have been a hectic blur. We sold our house and are now moved into our new home. The move went surprisingly smooth in spite of the last minute panic packing.

For the first few weeks, I felt very disoriented and unable to focus on anything. I was in a constant state of confusion. I finally feel more settled and at home now. I love the new house. It is so bright and open. I feel relaxed and at peace here. It feels like a fresh start.

My husband really likes the new house but misses the old neighborhood. My son Q misses having his studio and bedroom in the basement like he did in the old house. He is talking about getting his own apartment. My daughter J moved into her first apartment just before we moved into the new house. It is a huge adjustment to having one of my children no longer living at home. I miss her living with us, but I'm glad that she is happy in her new place. All I want is for both my kids to be healthy, safe and happy. My puppy Charlie loves the new house for numerous reasons; no grass yet means walks several times a day and the windows are unobscured since the shutters have not been installed yet which provides her with endless entertainment. As for me, I don't really miss the old house, maybe just the old studio space where I spent a lot of time working with Q, J and their band. We had a lot of fun during that time. I like the fresh start with the new house. My only regret is that my Dad will never see the new house and be part of the memories made there. But I think he would have liked the new house.

To be honest, I often wondered if I would live long enough to see the new house. When the pandemic first started here in March 2020 and everything got shut down, I was so scared for my family and for myself because of pre-existing conditions which put me at greater risk of dying if I caught the virus.

Everyday I still worry about my family's health and for good reason. The total number of Covid-19 cases worldwide today, September 29th 2020, are 33,732,181 with 7,695,382 active cases right now. Canada has a total of 156,655 cases with 13,969 active cases and 9,289 deaths. There are 1,009,512 deaths world-wide. We are starting the second wave and it looks like it's going to be a lot worse than the first one. I desperately want to see my Mom, and my Mother in-law and Father in-law, but the only way to keep them safe is to stay away from them so we don't bring them the virus if we are carrying it asymptomatically. It's a crazy, frightening time we are living in. We are all trying to stay safe by wearing masks and sanitizing our hands when we go out, but the fear of catching the virus is very real. Even a trip to the grocery store leaves me exhausted and worried. I never shop for fun anymore and I used to love shopping, along with going out for dinner and going to see a movie. I've been to only two restaurants in the past seven months and haven't been to a movie theatre in 8 months. I prefer to stay home and be safe. It's my safety nest. It's a crazy, frightening time we are living in. And I pray every night that this nightmare will be over soon.

Sincerely,

Jamie

Letter 36 — Relationships Change

Dear Jamie,

Thank you for sharing your encounters with your mom after your dad's death. I see a definite transformation in your feelings towards your mom. I smiled when you wrote about your "Dad's affairs". I knew you meant his physical belongings and not his romantic relationships with other women.

It is sad that Covid-19 has separated many family members living in different cities, sometimes even those living in the same city. Knowing that such a separation is indefinite and unpredictable makes it even harder. Human beings are social animals and we need physical and emotional touch to survive and thrive.

I think becoming a mother of your children also changed your relationship with your mom as a daughter. Our life experiences change us and our relationships in more ways than one.

I am happy that you are settling in your new house and you are transforming a house into a home. It is like starting a new chapter of your life.

I am glad your relationship with your mom and your children is becoming stronger.

Now I have a question for you. Many readers will wonder why you did not share the story of your sexual abuse with your mom.

Peacefully,

Dr. Sohail

Letter 37 — Why I Kept Silent

Dear Dr. Sohail,

My Mom and I have been very close for my whole life. She has always been there for me. But it took me until I was twenty eight years old to tell her about the abuse. There were several reasons for that.

The abuse started when I was very young so I was very traumatized by it. To ensure my silence, my abuser had threatened to kill me and my mother if I ever told. I believed him and was terrified of him. Fortunately for him, my mind blocked out the abuse while it was happening and then afterward, my mind blocked the memory of it. The abuse was not an isolated incident, but happened repeatedly over several years. My mind hid it all from me, even when I was old enough to understand what was happening. I just knew on a very deep level that something was horribly wrong but didn't know what it was. As a child I wanted to run away from home, but didn't know why. Then as a teenager, I started to get depressed and started thinking about suicide. In my mid-twenties, the depression became severe. By the time I was twenty six years old, I had been hospitalized three times for depression, suicidal ideation and suicide attempts. It wasn't until I ended up in the Psychotherapy Unit that I started to remember, through flashbacks and body memories, that I was abused as a child. Once I had recovered enough memories to piece together what had happened to me and who had abused me, I told my Mom and Dad. They were shocked but supportive.

I never told anyone else in my family about the abuse. My abuser had been dead for several years by the time I remembered so I didn't have to reveal the abuse to protect others from him. Also I did not think anyone in my family would believe me and I didn't want to hurt my parents who would have suffered the backlash for my revealing the abuse. I also did not want to hurt my sweet, loving, gentle grandmother who would have been devastated to learn that I had been hurt. I couldn't do it. I had paid a big enough price for his abuse; I wasn't going to let my parents and Grandma pay the price too. They didn't deserve that.

In some ways I'm still paying for the abuse even though it's been twenty five years since I remembered it. The flashbacks and body memories are rare these days but some of the beliefs and feelings that resulted from the abuse are still prevalent. I still struggle at times with self-esteem and self-confidence. And I still get depressed at times, but the depression is not as strong and does not last as long as it did before. I bounce back faster. Although believing that I matter and have worth can be a bit of a struggle still for me, at my core I now believe those things. Even though I value myself now more than ever, I still struggle with putting myself first. I have no problem putting my family first though, especially my children.

Sincerely,

Jamie

Letter 38 — The Importance of A Trusting Therapeutic Relationship

Dear Jamie,

Your letter is very important for the readers, whether they are patients or therapists. It highlights how painful and traumatic experiences remain buried in the deep recesses of the unconscious mind for weeks, months, years, even decades and surface from time to time as depressive thoughts and suicidal ideas until a patient has an opportunity to create a trusting therapeutic relationship with a kind, caring and compassionate therapist. That is when deeply buried memories come to the surface to be processed in therapy. That is when the patient starts to recover. You are lucky that you had an opportunity to heal and grow. It is profoundly sad that there are so many young women who suffer all their lives and never find a caring therapist.

Peacefully,

Dr. Sohail

Letter 39 — My World

Dear Dr. Sohail,

Sorry about the long delay since my last letter. The overall stress from the move and the constant worry about my family's health during this pandemic is starting to take a toll on my mental health. I often wake up in the middle of the night in a panic that someone I love will get sick or worse. My daughter is a nurse and not able to be isolated. My son is still trying to build his music career and has to work outside the home at times. I'm terrified that they will get sick. My mom is isolating alone with just her dog for companionship. My in-laws are isolating too. My husband and I are isolating and limiting trips out of the house. With my pre-existing conditions, I know I'm at higher risk for death if I contract Covid-19. Ironically, after all the years that I spent suicidal, I'm not ready to die yet. I want to see my kids get married and have children of their own. I'm looking forward to having a grandchild some day.

This constant worry is chipping away at the initial joy that I felt over the new house which I really like. It's draining me emotionally and mentally. I'm getting depressed. Just trying to think to write is the equivalent of swimming through thick mud. It's been a real struggle. I'm starting to shut down emotionally. I can't feel. I can't write. I'm numb. Most days have been spent just trying to motivate myself to clean the kitchen, empty the dishwasher and then if i have any energy left try to unpack just one box. Today I did something that I haven't done in a very long time, and it was greatly needed. I turned on the music from my youth and listened. With each song, memories started to flood in along with intense emotion. It felt like a switch had been flipped. Now I honestly just want to curl up on the couch in a ball and cry. I feel worried, scared, confused and guilty. But at least I'm able to feel and since I can feel, I can now write.

Writing about my kids is really tough for me. I love them so much and they mean the entire world to me. Words just don't seem to be adequate enough to describe how I feel about them. I would easily give my life for them in a heartbeat.

I'm so proud of both my kids! They have grown into responsible, honest, kind, compassionate, hard working and very intelligent adults. I love them dearly! They are not afraid to take risks and don't back down from a challenge. They are everything I had hoped they would become when I held them as infants in my arms.

Sincerely,

Jamie

Letter 40 — Pandemic Stress

Dear Jamie,

The Corona Virus (Covid – 19) pandemic has been stressful for so many people in so many ways especially for those families whose members live in different cities and provinces, countries and continents. Some of my patients feel imprisoned in their own homes, while others feel isolated from their dear ones because of travel restrictions and lockdowns. It is also ironic that people living under the same roof have different expectations from each other. Some like to follow the rules strictly while others are relaxed about them. There are others who feel controlled by obsessive relatives, even children.

I received my first dose of Moderna vaccine, hoping that I would be able to travel by the end of 2021 and see my family in Pakistan. In 2020 I had to cancel my vacations in March 2020 as well as October 2020 because of travel restrictions. Even now my niece Wardah has been stranded in Pakistan as the flights got cancelled two hours before her flight back to Canada.

I am hopeful that as more and more Canadians get vaccinated and the numbers of Covid – 19 cases go down we will be able to socialize, eat out and travel. Let us hope that life evolves to a new normal soon.

Peacefully,

Dr. Sohail

Letter 41 —The Nest Is Empty

Dear Dr. Sohail,

The day I was dreading has finally arrived; my youngest child has left the nest. My son Q got his own apartment in Toronto with his best friend. The house is so quiet and feels empty. I feel lost. I think my pup Charlie feels lost too. We both really miss Q. I think my husband does too even though he doesn't say much about it. When my daughter J moved out, it was a big adjustment for us, but at least she moved into an apartment close by and visited regularly. I miss J. We spent a lot of time together. I'm now missing Q too. When he was home, the house was noisy, but in a good way. Now it's so quiet.

The silence weighs down on me and reminds me that the child-rearing stage of my life is officially over. I grieve for the days when the kids were young and I could still carry them in my arms. My arms feel empty. I miss helping with homework, the hectic after school events, the nightly bedtime rituals, and weekend outings. Their childhoods ended so quickly that I barely noticed those final days were winding down. Before I knew it, they didn't want me to tuck them in every night, then they didn't want to watch TV with me, then they were too busy to sit and chat. Their childhoods went by too fast. It feels like it was another lifetime.

Up until Q moved out, my days were still structured around his schedule somewhat. I would see what Q had planned for his day and plan to spend time with him, even if it was a quick cup of tea. We would spend time talking about his music career. Now I barely know what is going on with his career. He is the captain of his own ship now. I feel adrift. My last anchor of motherhood has been severed. I'm still a mom, but not a hands-on one, just to my dog Charlie. The end of the role of mother is jaring. I don't know how to define myself any more. Even though J is really busy these days with her new job and with her boyfriend, we still hangout when she is available but it feels more like hanging out with a friend, than a mother-child. I honestly don't know who I am now, but I think it's time for me to find out who I am and what I want.

When I first became a mother, someone told me that the best thing a parent can do for their child is to work themselves out of that job. A successful parent will ensure that their child can confidently and willingly go into the world on their own and thrive; they no longer need the parent. I guess I succeeded twice. I never wanted my children to cling to me in fear of the world or feel that they could not live without me. I always wanted for them to confidently strike out on their own and seek their independence with confidence, determination and bravery. And J and Q have both done that and I am so very proud of them. I'm excited to see their future successes, celebrate their joys and support them through difficult times too. I'm hoping to be blessed with grandchildren one day.

For now though, I will allow myself to mourn the end of their childhood and my role as a hands-on mother. I will be kind to myself and not berate myself when I feel sad.

I know it will take time for me to adapt to this huge change in my life.

Sincerely,

Jamie

Letter 42 — Graduation

Dear Jamie,

You are feeling sad as your children are leaving home and you are experiencing a loss.

I would like to see that experience from a different angle. I want to congratulate you that you played the role of a mother successfully. Your children leaving home and starting a new and independent life on their own can be seen as a graduation for you as a mother. I know many grown up children in their twenties and thirties and even forties who never left home. They are still financially, emotionally and socially dependent on their parents who are getting old and fragile. Some of those parents have become senior citizens and worry about the future of their dependent, grown up children when they are no longer in this world.

You are lucky to see your children fly high right in front of your eyes.

Dr. K Sohail and Jamie Lochlan

They trust your love and know that when they need you, you will welcome them with open arms and heart.

Peacefully,

Dr. Sohail

Letter 43 — Friend Or Forget It

Dear Dr. Sohail,

As I wander around this very quiet house, I feel lonely. My husband is upstairs working and it's just me and Charlie. J and Q come for visits but it's not the same. And it will never be the same.

I ask myself "Who is Jamie and what does she want" but the answers don't come easily. I know right now I want to be less lonely. I feel like I don't really have any friends. I have a few acquaintances, but no true friends. My best friend from highschool passed away a few years ago. I miss her. My one friend N lives too far away so we talk very infrequently on the phone. I'm trying to make a new friend S, but it's difficult when we can't see each other and get to really know each other because of the lockdowns. I look back on my life and wonder why I have no friends. There is no one to blame but me, and it's a sad realization. I tried to make friends, but it was never something that came easily. I think it was multiple problems that hindered my ability to make friends.

The first major problem to overcome when making friends is establishing trust. Since I was abused by someone close to me, my trust was betrayed on such a deep level that it affected my ability to trust others. Superficial relationships are easy, but making a deep, trusting relationship is very difficult for me. My defences kick in and my walls go up, making it very difficult for both me and a potential friend to break through.

The second problem when I did make a friend was it always seemed that I valued the friendship more than they did. They were always too busy to spend time with me and eventually they just drifted away or I walked away out of frustration. I got tired of being told I didn't matter and was not worthy of even a few minutes of their time. One lesson I've learned is that people make time for what is important to them. If someone keeps telling you they are too busy to spend even a few minutes with you, then what they are really saying is that you don't matter to them. Message received. This happened a lot to me so eventually I just found it easier to not even try and make friends.

The third problem was my low self-esteem. When friends were too busy to connect, it was easy for me to believe that the friend didn't value me because I didn't value myself in the relationship. My low self-esteem made it difficult to even try to make friends and it left me in a very lonely place. A place I no longer want to be in.

Once it's safe to be around people outside of one's household, I plan on putting a conscious effort into making friends, including building new friendships with S and N. But I'm promising myself now that I will not accept any friendships that are one-sided. I'm done being told that I'm not worth another person's time. If they feel that way, I don't want to be friends with them. I deserve better. I'll also explore new hobbies and interests. Maybe now it's time for me. I'll find out who Jamie is and what she wants. My children taught me to be patient, to be kind, to be brave and to love. Now I need to apply those lessons to myself. Another major lesson that raising my children taught me is that time is precious and short. Cherish it, use it and don't waste it because the future becomes the present a lot faster than you realize.

Sincerely,

Jamie

Letter 44 — Green Zone

Dear Jamie,

Now that your children have flown away from the nest, you have an opportunity to focus on your own desires and ambitions and dreams. Let me share some ideas and ideals that I shared last week in my Green zone Seminar for Green Zone Community members. I hope they inspire you to have some initiates for your new life.

Peacefully,

Dr. Sohail

THREE ROADS TO GREEN ZONE LIFESTYLE

Today we had a Green Zone Seminar, the fifth of the series.

We discussed three roads to a peaceful Green Zone Lifestyle.

- o Creating
- o Sharing
- o Serving

I shared with our Green Zone Community members who attended the seminar that according to Green Zone Philosophy every child is born with special gift. It is the responsibility of parents and teachers to help the children recognize and then nurture those special gifts so that children can grow to their full potential.

According to Green Zone Philosophy there are three parts to our personality.

Every child is born with a Natural Self, a sum total of all the potential.

Because of social, religious and cultural conditioning a part of the Natural transforms into Conditioned Self that is guided by what that person

- o should do
- o must do
- o have to do

Another part of Natural Self transforms into Creative self that is guided what that person would

- o like to do
- o want to do
- o love to do

Creative Self is connected with that person's special gifts.

When special gifts are nurtured they express themselves as hobbies and grow into passions and then transform into dreams.

When a Green Zone Lifestyle is accomplished then those creative dreams come true.

When I was a teenager I realized that life had given me two special gifts: a gift of writing and a gift of healing.

So I became a writer and a psychotherapist to create my Green Zone Lifestyle.

The second road to Green Zone Lifestyle is Sharing.

After recognizing and expressing our Creative Self, we enjoy it more if we share our creative gifts with our dear ones and also with like-minded people.

I share my gift of writing with my creative and writer friends that I call my Family of the Heart. They enjoy my poems and stories and essays and give me positive and constructive feedback.

The third road to Green Zone Lifestyle is Serving.

I encourage my clients to do some voluntary work and pay back to the community for all the gifts of love they had received throughout their lives from all the near and dear ones. By helping others we help ourselves.

I share with my clients and colleagues that my serving my community and humanity include

- o writing articles for internet HUM SUB magazine
- o doing interviews with Dr. Baland Iqbal for Canada One TV program IN SEARCH OF WISDOM that can be found on Youtube
- o offering Green Zone Seminars for the Green Zone Community of more than 1200 members. That is my humble contribution to mental health education that our community desperately needs as so many men and women and children have been silently suffering for so many years and decades and not getting professional help that they need.

Over the years and decades I have discovered two secrets of happiness:

Passion and Compassion

I express my passion in my creative writing and I express my compassion by doing creative psychotherapy in my clinic.

My Green Zone Lifestyle consists of three parts to my creative triangle:

- o Creative Writing
- o Creative Psychotherapy
- o Creative Friends.

I spend my days doing creative psychotherapy in my clinic, my evenings with my creative friends and my weekends reading and doing creative reading and writing.

For me Green Zone Living is *peaceful living*.

I feel fortunate that I am able to teach what I practice and practice what I teach.

My Green Zone Philosophy makes my life purposeful and meaningful.

Letter 45 — Not Broken

Dear Dr. Sohail

For the longest time, I thought of myself as permanently broken. I didn't think that I could ever heal from the trauma of the abuse. The wounds were too deep and severe. I thought that the recurring depression and suicidal thoughts were proof that I would never heal. But I was wrong!

I don't think of myself as broken anymore. Wounded yes, healing yes, but not broken. The depression was a long term consequence of the abuse. The suicidal thoughts were a byproduct of the depression and response to it that had been fueled by the belief that I didn't matter and I was worthless. Those beliefs were at my core and I had to learn in therapy that I do matter and that I have worth. Your encouragement, patience and gentle guidance, and your willingness to stand by me taught me that I matter and that I have worth. Thank you.

Although I still fall into depression sometimes, it doesn't last long, or go as deep as before. But more importantly, I know that because of your ongoing support, and the hard work that I've done in therapy that I will get through the depression. I know that life is worth living even when it's difficult.

When you first suggested writing this book together, I was worried that I wouldn't be able to do it for a few reasons. Writer to writer, I didn't want to disappoint you. I value our connection as writers and it was this connection initially that allowed me to start trusting you and let us build a safe, trusting, therapeutic relationship. I know there are times in my life when I can't write so I didn't know if I could complete the project. I need the highs and lows of extreme emotion to be able to write, but sometimes I'm numb and simply can't write. And I can't write when I'm happy or content. I need intense emotion. The death of the singer of my favorite band from my childhood triggered past memories of me as a child listening to his music to escape the reality of the abuse and the awful feelings that it brought up. Then Q moving out really pushed me into overdrive with intense emotion and a flood of memories of his and J's childhood. Now I can finally write again and it feels like being able to breathe again.

I was also hesitant to write this book because I didn't know if I could take that hard look at my past and write about it again. I used excerpts from my novel "Shore of Nowhere" (marked with an asterisk *) that captured that time in my life when I first started remembering the abuse because it was exactly what I needed to share with our readers in the most honest way possible. I plan on releasing "Shore of Nowhere," along with a few poetry books, because I feel that it's finally time I tell my story and express my feelings. I'm telling my story here in the hope that it will help someone who is struggling with depression, suicidal thoughts and issues of abuse and trauma. If this book helps just one person, then it's all worth it. For anyone reading this book, I just want to say, *YOU ARE WORTH IT! YOU MATTER!* Be kind to yourself, you deserve it. You don't have to go through this alone; find a caring, compassionate therapist or friend to help you, and reach out for help, especially when you are at your lowest point. You deserve their kindness, compassion and empathy.

I also want to tell readers not to let the labels that others put on you define you. They are a guide for treatment; not a life sentence. It's your life and you get to decide how you live it. When I was first admitted to the hospital and waiting to be transferred to the Psychotherapy Unit, the very kind and compassionate unit psychiatrist said that my diagnosis was Reactive Depression, Obsessive Compulsive Disorder, and Personality Disorder. But he stated that he didn't truly believe that it was Personality Disorder but something else that hopefully would be uncovered during my on-going therapy. This psychiatrist truly wanted to help me. And thanks to him I was finally on the right path to getting the help that I needed. With the intense therapy, the real reason behind my depression emerged. The Personality Disorder diagnosis was removed and replaced with Post Traumatic Stress Disorder from childhood sexual abuse. Years later, while starting my therapy with Dr. Sohail, I learned that I suffer from Cyclothymia, which is the mildest form of Bipolar Disorder. I reluctantly agreed to take medication and as a result, the mood swings became manageable. The medication helped level me out and kept me from sliding back into severe depression. I took the medication for several years, but I've been off it for over a year and a half now and I'm still managing the mood swings without any issues. I'm also happy to say that I have not been hospitalized since being in the Psychotherapy Unit over twenty five years ago.

Although it was a long and difficult journey, I'm finally in a place where I accept my past. I have compassion for myself, especially for my inner child who was so horribly abused. I feel and honor her pain. Issues still arise at times, but I can put them aside, live my life and deal with them when I choose. My day to day life is not affected by my past. I also know that I need to listen to my gut and trust it, even when my brain is overriding it. I trust myself now and on a deeper level than I have before. I'm healing.

I am so very grateful to the Psychotherapy Unit, especially to my prime and associate therapists (who I gave the pseudonyms Kathy and Beth in both novels to protect their identities). They literally saved my life and enabled me to have a life worth living. I will forever be grateful for their caring, kindness and compassion that made a huge difference in my young life. I will always remember my time with them with fondness.

And to my family, I'm so thankful for all of them. They are my heart and my reason for facing my past and dealing with it so that I can still be here for them. They mean the world to me and are still my motivation for everything. I'm also so very grateful to you, Dr. Sohail, for all your support over the years. I could not have survived without your weekly support, encouragement and insight. Thank you for encouraging me to write. Writer to writer, I'm very proud to co-author this book with you, and I have tremendous respect for you as a writer and therapist. Thank you for everything.

Sincerely,

Jamie

Letter 46 — Creative Psychotherapy

Dear Jamie,

I would like to congratulate you in completing this creative and therapeutic project. Now we are co-authors of this wonderful book reflecting the essence of creative psychotherapy.

The credit of this book goes mostly to you. It was your story. I was a catalyst who was prompting you with my letters.

Over the years, I have seen you heal and grow and become more self aware and more confident. Your self esteem, self image and self confidence have grown enormously.

Now I can present you as a role model to our readers who will be inspired by your story. They will think, `` If Jamie can do it, we can do it too."

I am so proud of your emotional achievements and creative accomplishments.

I hope you feel confident enough now that you publish your previous poems and stories that you were reluctant to share before because of your insecurities and apprehensions. Let the sun of your creativity shine and let more and more people benefit from your creative gifts. That will help you create a circle of creative friends, your family of the heart.

When our joint book is published it will become a creative bridge between you and your readers and you can present it as a gift to your dear ones. You will be happy when you see a smile of gratitude on their faces. I can already imagine you autographing the books and people taking pictures with you and your book.

Peacefully,

Dr. Sohail

Dear Readers,

Please feel free to check out Dr. Sohail's **Green Zone Living** (greenzoneliving.ca) website along with his books on Green Zone Living series available on amazon.com and amazon.ca

After reading this book feel free to share your comments and suggestions as your feedback will help us make necessary changes in the future editions of this book.

Dr. Sohail: email address:
welcome@drsohail.com

For more written books by Jamie Lochlan, please search amazon.ca and amazon.com or join her email list at jamielochlan.author@gmail.com

www.ingramcontent.com/pod-product-compliance
Lightning Source LLC
Chambersburg PA
CBHW021618270326
41931CB00008B/749